MW01194567

Book provided
by the

FRIENDS of the **STATE LIBRARY** and
ARCHIVES of **FLORIDA**

ADVANCE PRAISE

"Articulating goals in words is valuable but visualizing a desired state and how to get there has been a powerful unlock for our team at Brooks. Whether your aspirations are personal or shared, Dobrowolski's *Drawing Your Future* will help you create clarity and tangible dimension for your world of possibility."

—DAN SHERIDAN, CEO, Brooks Running Co.

"Patti Dobrowolski's Drawing Your Future process helped me to transform my life. Over the past decade, I've manifested every aspect of my vision. This creative guidebook offers the tools to harness your visual thinking and make you the most powerful change agent in realizing your dreams."

—TIFFANY DUFU, Bestselling author, podcaster, inspirator, and president of the Tory Burch Foundation

"For many people, making change can be incredibly scary. But when Patti Dobrowolski shows you how to use a picture to help you, you'll become a change genie standing before a magic road map to your future. I've seen this process help countless entrepreneurs succeed—this book will truly change your life."

—CHAITRA VEDULLAPALLI, Cofounder and president, Women in Cloud

"As the cofounder of Chief, I have witnessed firsthand the incredible impact that Dobrowolski's work has on women leaders. Her experiential visioning process is a game-changer, empowering you to draw pictures to brainstorm and activate your future with confidence and bold steps. In *Drawing Your Future*, her hands-on practical tools will enable anyone to harness the power of visual thinking, turning ideas into action and vision into reality."

—LINDSAY KAPLAN, Cofounder of Chief, investment partner at Next Wave, startup advisor, and *Forbes* columnist

"Dobrowolski has written a short-cut guide to help you uplevel your ability to facilitate getting what you need or want by using pictures. Visualizing success is key to making it happen, and this book is packed with visual solution strategies to help you brainstorm better, envision, and activate a powerful future and pitch any idea for your next venture. I do not have great drawing skills, but I have learned through this book that this doesn't matter. Having personally practiced and experienced this unique visual process, I was able to clearly see my map to the future and then make it happen. No matter your drawing skill, this book will up your innovation game!"

—GAVRIELLA SCHUSTER, Board director, global business executive, and TEDx speaker

"In my early years of career navigation, I used Patti's Draw Your Future process and was totally inspired by the results I got by attaching myself to my future using a picture. I immediately showed her TEDx Talk to my managers and company to inspire others to ambition their career. *Drawing Your Future* has transformed my own ability to envision and helped my followers envision their success."

—JONATHAN JAVIER, CEO and founder, Wonsulting

"Like having coffee
with an expert"

ALSO BY
PATTI DOBROWOLSKI

Creative Genius You: The Equation That Makes YOU Great

9 Tips to Up Your Creative Genius

*Drawing Solutions: How Visual Goal Setting
Will Change Your Life*

DRAWING YOUR FUTURE

Solve Problems
Explain Ideas
Sell Anything

BY PATTI DOBROWOLSKI

IDEAPRESS
PUBLISHING

WASHINGTON, DC

IDEAPRESS
PUBLISHING

Ideapress Publishing | **www.ideapresspublishing.com**

All trademarks are the property of their respective companies.
Cover Design by Victoria Kim
Cover Photo by David Hamilton
Illustrations by Patti Dobrowolski and Scott Ward
Cataloging-in-Publication Data is on file with the Library of Congress.
ISBN: 978-1-64687-167-4

Special Sales
Ideapress books are available at a special discount for bulk purchases for sales promotions and premiums, or for use in corporate training programs. Special editions, including personalized covers, a custom foreword, corporate imprints, and bonus content are also available.

Non-Obvious® is a registered trademark of the Influential Marketing Group.

1 2 3 4 5 6 7 8 9 10

DEDICATION

To Julie Boardman, who fills my world with moving vans,
adopted pets, and unexpected adventures.

If you want to learn how to draw and achieve exceptional results, this book is a must-read for you. One of the biggest challenges we face in today's hybrid world is our inability to focus. This book will guide you on how to grab a pen, take a step toward the paper, and confidently draw ideas. It will teach you how to map solutions and help others focus on key results, enabling them to step into their future faster.

PART TWO—EXPLAIN ANYTHING USING
PICTURES

Chapter 4

How to See Things Better

PART THREE—USING PICTURES TO UNPACK
AND EVOLVE ANYTHING

Chapter 5

Ouch, That Challenge Hurts:
Leverage It to Set the Stage to Win

PUBLISHER'S NOTE

Is This Guide for You?

If you picked up this book, you are not a dummy. Many business guides treat you like an idiot. Some even say so on the cover. This is not one of those books.

The first time I experienced Patti's captivating approach to explaining ideas, she was in front of a digital whiteboard, enthusiastically transforming complex concepts into memorable visuals. Patti is celebrated for this unique talent, but what truly sets her apart is her genuine passion for sharing her methods with others. *Drawing Your Future* isn't just about artistic skill; it's about being more persuasive by visualizing your ideas. With Patti as your guide, this book will help you discover how to unlock your creative potential and bring any idea to life.

ROHIT BHARGAVA
Founder, Non-Obvious Guides
2x TEDx Speaker + Keynote Speaker at 300+ Events

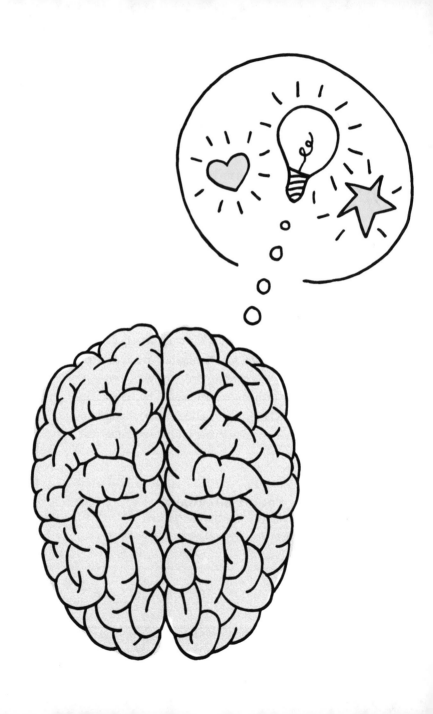

In this book,
you will learn . . .

- ✔ Why drawing pictures is needed now more than ever

- ✔ How to rekindle your relationship with drawing and wield a marker with ease

- ✔ How to capture quickly to uncover better solutions

- ✔ How to extricate the problem

- ✔ How to draw out possible solutions

- ✔ How to link concepts for insights

- ✔ Ways to sell your big ideas

- ✔ How to fuel dreams with positivity

Introduction

Hi, I'm Patti. I usually describe myself as a live illustrator, keynote speaker, and change agent. But the truth is, I am obsessed with how to make change happen faster. I'm not the one wringing their hands when it comes to change. I thrive in times of change, especially when it becomes uncomfortable.

Why? Because change stretches me. I have had three very successful careers—first as an actor who made it to Broadway, then as a change agent and visual facilitator working in business for thirty years, and now as an author and keynote speaker.

I have helped teams make changes from the front line to the C-suite across all industries. I created my signature process, Draw Your Future (DYF), to help myself and others get unstuck during change. Initially, I didn't know why it worked, but eventually, the brain science substantiated what I had seen happen in meetings time and again. The truth? A picture helps you make change better. Maya Angelou once said, "A solitary fantasy can totally transform one million realities." I know for a fact that a picture can transform at least one reality—*yours*.

In 2011, I delivered a TEDx Talk called "Draw Your Future." I rehearsed that talk for six weeks, and when I stepped into that red circle, I nailed it. The talk was viewed not just on the regular TEDx channel but was also picked up in a Best of 2015 series, where it got nearly six million views. As I went through the comments, I realized that the audience was intrigued by the notion that a simple drawing could empower them to change their future.

Everyone dreams of a better future and yearns to achieve their goals quickly, so drawing one's future seems like a fantastic idea. However, many people believe they cannot draw. The most common comment I receive is, "My drawing skills suck."

Since my teenage years, I've been curious about how we can propel ourselves into the future and effect change more rapidly. In my thirties, I discovered that imagining my future and taking action toward it by drawing a picture helped me make it happen faster.

Since that time, I have been training myself to draw everything, whether I am describing a concept or illustrating a company's five-year vision and strategy. What I have discovered through over thirty years of research is that whatever you depict sticks. Hand drawing captivates and inspires better thinking because drawing makes the thinking visible.

This form of magic found me when I started my adult life as a solo performer writing and performing short plays that involved multiple characters. In those early years, I never had the financial independence or the freedom to take many vacations to explore the world. So, I was obsessed with my inner world and what I could create using my imagination. I'd read enough Einstein to know there were ways to break through the time-space continuum, and I was determined to find them. I had evidence that it was possible when, as a performer, I held a picture in my mind of myself on Broadway and sketched out a few drawings of me on that stage, and within a year, that picture manifested.

Years later, when I had gone back to get a graduate degree and began to work in the corporate sector, I sat in a brainstorming meeting with one of the first visualizers, Gordon Rudow. He was a skilled quick drawer, and with a piece of paper on the office walls, he wrote and drew our consulting team's discussion and created a "vision" of our core ideas.

The process inspired me, and though I was not a visual artist by any means, I was determined to learn how to do it. It looked fun, and it captured everyone's attention in the room in ways that, with my limited business experience, I wasn't able to yet. It was like a bright and shiny portal to my future beckoning me, so I grabbed a pen and walked through it.

Since the day I started, I have been working with businesses, both big and small, across the globe to turn their vision and strategy into visual representations. With pen, paper, and pastels in my hand, I honed my drawing skills and became the "Wizard at the Whiteboard." Each year, as I got better, I became more and more passionate about showing others how to use their natural doodling skills to capture their ideas and expand their future.

I mentioned earlier that neuroscience eventually confirmed what was already evident—drawing pictures helps us solve problems more efficiently. By taking the risk of putting pen to paper and drawing your ideas and strategies, you'll embark on an engaging, flow-filled journey, having more fun than ever before. That is, once you push your critic aside, so let's start there. Critic, take a seat!

PART ONE

Why Drawing Matters

CHAPTER 1

How to Get the Best Out of Your Brain

Every morning, when you wake up and start your day, you have a mental picture of what it will look like. Maybe you imagine your feet hitting the floor, your first cup of coffee, or your computer turning on. All these things are an automated function and a repeat of yesterday's neural network. All of us play the same record on our old-school turntable, often repeating the exact same song. While it may seem like we have chosen a different tune, trust me when I say we are stuck in a repetitive cycle of behavior and thinking.

Why? Well, this cycle is comfortable, easy, unchallenging, and consistent, and it only engages the familiar parts of our brains. The version of you that is more capable and achieving greater success with your goals exists in the future, which is unknown. However, you can access a higher level of awareness when you create visual representations. You need only draw a picture.

1.1	**Your Brain and Its Unique Visual Language: The Innate Picture-Making Ability of Your Brain**

Your brain is made up of a whole bunch of different parts that you can ask ChatGPT about to learn more. But there are three parts I am going to cover here:

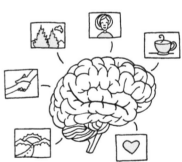

1. The cerebellum, which is the part of your brain known as the "little brain" and helps you with muscle control, language, and memory

2. The hippocampus, which is the part of your brain that plays an important role in the process of learning and the formation of new memories

3. The prefrontal cortex, which is the part of your brain that helps you orchestrate thoughts and actions to achieve your goals for the future

Your hippocampus is an image maker because the brain spends its time making pictures of experiences and feelings before storing them in the vast warehouse of your memories. It's essentially a picture-making machine. It processes approximately seventy-four gigabytes of data every day, 90 percent of which are pictures. Your brain chooses to keep some images and to discard others. The

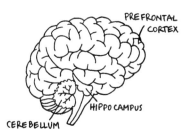

memories that remain are determined by the amount of feeling attached to them—either positive or negative.

> When you have a powerful experience, it is like taking a highlighter pen to that experience.

Good or bad, that day, time, place, person, or object is covered with a bright yellow marker, subsequently stored in the hippocampus, and then used by your neocortex whenever you unconsciously or consciously trigger it.

When you want to create a different future or expand your capacity to do, sell, or develop something, you can heighten your access to that possible future when you draw a picture of it.

1.2 Human Nature and Pictures: Images Unlock Your Genius by Leveraging Human Nature

Let's learn a little more about why drawing stuff matters.

> Since your brain is an innate picture-making machine, each time you see, feel, or do something that your brain deems memorable, it creates a full-color children's book of the moment.

Once created, at any time, you can open that book and flip through the pages to relive it.

Earlier I mentioned your automated morning ritual. The brain runs these old tapes to prevent you from becoming completely exhausted. It follows the path of least resistance so you can save your strength for the bigger challenges to come. Challenges like learning new things, brainstorming new ideas, and solving problems, all of which require you to create new neural pathways, which then drains your energy stores. This is just one of the reasons why meeting break times are filled with sugary snacks to restore all the glucose you burned up thinking. Your brain is *hungry* after you have used it.

While actively listening to others or engaging in life's challenges, you are essentially pulling up images, mixing and matching them, keeping some, and discarding others to come up with solutions.

Sorting through images to get to the good stuff is where drawing comes in handy.

In fact, I'm sure you know that you are more likely to remember what you are reading right now if you draw pictures of the content. In the first good study about using visuals, researchers found that you remember 30 percent better the information that you draw.[1] That may not seem like a lot, but it is if you consider your future depends on it.

Even when you draw a bad picture, you are more likely to remember it. In a Princeton study, researchers showed a group two sets of information—one written in a beautiful font and one in an ugly font.[2] Weirdly enough, the subjects remembered the data in the ugly font better. For those of you who are thinking, "Good thing because I can only draw stick figures," you already have a leg up on the rest of us who are confident with drawing! (Let the competition begin!)

IF YOU WANT TO TEST YOUR BRAIN'S CAPACITY TO REMEMBER, USE AN UGLY FONT.

1.3 The Not-So-Hidden Secret of Drawing: Why Pictures Tell a Better Story

RECYCLE   COMPOST   LANDFILL

Pictures have become the new gold in the world of social media. Recent research suggests that by adding a picture or video to social media posts, you can increase the number of views by as much as 70 percent.[3] Due to the overwhelming amount of information we consume daily—from our internet feeds to the movies we watch, the ads we see, and the things we shop for—our brains are bombarded with a huge volume of data. It is crucial to develop the ability to filter out irrelevant information to concentrate on what is truly important. Otherwise, you may end up feeling overloaded and exhausted, which happens when you spend too much time thinking without taking a break.

Even though you might be aware of this fact, it's worth emphasizing that the most effective way to absorb information is to read or work on it in twenty-minute intervals and then take breaks. That's why it's advisable to pause right now and draw a picture of what you've just read.

While you might think that your brain is always coming up with fresh ideas, when you start to brainstorm, it starts by accessing the backwash of your memory. To get to the new ideas, you must break out of the patterns of your past. A simple way to do that is to draw a picture.

Drawing a picture will highlight what's important for your brain, and ugly drawings are remembered even better.

CHAPTER SUMMARY
KEY TAKEAWAYS:

- Drawing a picture highlights what's important for your brain and increases your memory by 30 percent.

- The uglier a font or drawing, the higher the chance of remembering it.

- The brain is a pattern-making machine that can be disrupted by artistic change, such as drawing a picture or listening to different music.

CHAPTER 2

Why Drawing Your Future Helps You Solve Anything

2.1   The Future You: Attaching Yourself to a Future You

The phone rang, and I saw an unknown number. My initial thought was that it might be a spam call, but I decided to answer it anyway. A woman introduced herself as Sheryl from the Consumer Financial Protection Bureau and asked how I was doing. My first instinct was to worry that someone had hacked my credit. However, she explained that they were interested in using the Draw Your Future (DYF) process to help people save money for their future. Professor Hal Hershfield from UCLA was conducting a study and wanted to include my process. Of course, I wanted to participate! But first, I wanted to hear more from Dr. Hershfield, so I flew to LA to meet him at his office.

During my conversation with Hal regarding his research, he shared an interesting insight. He explained that by visualizing yourself in the future and attaching yourself to that future version of yourself, you could improve your current actions and behaviors in relation to achieving a goal. The stronger the connection the better your desire and follow through to save more money, to care for your health, and to feel more successful in your life. In fact, studies showed that people with that strong connection actually saved 35 percent more money for their future.[4] An often-cited study by Dr. Gail Matthews, a psychology professor at Dominican University of California, shows the true power of writing down your goals. In a study with men and women, ages 23 to 72, from around the world and all walks of life (entrepreneurs, educators, health care professionals, artists, lawyers, and bankers), Matthews found people are 42 percent more likely to achieve goals and dreams by writing them down daily.[5]

But without this strong connection, we often don't achieve the goals we set. In fact, 88 percent of New Year's resolutions that are set are not achieved. This is why many of us have given up on making them.[6] We start motivated, but by mid-February, we've abandoned our goals and are left paying for a gym membership we never use until we eventually give up and cancel it in June.

When you attach yourself to an imagined "future you," it improves your actions in the here and now. You solve your problems with a more lasting impact. Learning this helped me make sense of the thousands of emails I received after the "Draw Your Future" TEDx Talk went viral on that bootleg channel.

People who had found success using the process had three things in common:

1. They could imagine a future self.

2. They believed that future self was a possibility.

3. They took small, consistent actions toward their future self's goals, and it helped them overcome the obstacles they had been facing.

That's when I discovered the value of marketing to a future you to see what's possible.

2.2 Market to Future You: What You Begin to Believe When You Picture a Future You

Marketing is a powerful tool that can influence our minds in ways we don't even realize. Pictures, as you know, are used to manipulate our thought process into desiring certain products. My favorite ads are from BMW, which does a great job of getting me to want the luxury and exclusivity of their branded cars. If ads can target our brains to make decisions, why can't we use the same strategy to target our brains to make better choices about our future?

Vision boards are a fairly well-known example of using pictures to create a storyboard of one's desired future. You cut out pictures of things you desire, glue them onto a piece of cardboard, and end up with a visual representation of your goals. I've done it quite successfully in the past, but then I discovered how to level up this practice—drawing your future.

Drawing a picture of your future is an even better tool for visualization because it helps you see what actually needs to change in your current life. It also engages both your visual and somatic senses. When you draw, the feelings spread throughout your body, and then you attach your feelings to the images you draw. When you dream and draw the future, it's a somatic level up that helps you feel the emotions associated with aspects of the future you desire. And it's an interactive process because as you draw the image, much like you did when you were a child, you begin to have fun.

The fun part opens your creativity and receptivity. Even the most basic shapes imprint themselves on your brain because you both see and experience them using imagination. The drawing stimulates your imagination and helps you to run thought experiments like Einstein did.

> Your brain takes a concept and experiments with different ideas and possibilities until you get lost in it and draw and dream a new reality. It's a flow experience that helps you to achieve a breakthrough result.

By envisioning a future that you desire, you encode your neural pathways with what it could look like and how it would feel when you achieve it. Simultaneously, you begin to detach from your past as your imagination runs wild with images of your desired outcome—whether it's fame, a fancy car, or publishing a book. Each daydream that you turn into a reality in your mind sends dopamine into your system, giving you a success high. This chemical reaction makes you feel invincible, and it happens every time you daydream about a positive future.

You are your own best marketer—more effective than any ad on social media. Now, what does that drawing do? It markets future you to present you each time you look at it. This reroutes your beliefs about your future, which reroutes your desire to take action to achieve it.

2.3 Attach Yourself to Future You: Proven Tips to Get Better Results When Goal Setting

In a business setting, you may wonder how you can use the Draw Your Future process with your team without getting laughed at for drawing bad pictures. Before you get worried, let me share some data from the big pharma company Hoffmann-La Roche (Roche). They studied the process with their pharma division and found that less than 40 percent of their team knew about the company's vision and strategy before having a visual picture of their future. However, after drawing the vision, strategy, and values into a picture, 96 percent of the team reported that they knew what the vision was, and 84 percent understood how what they did every day contributed to that vision. So, using visuals to convey important information can be a powerful tool for effective communication in a business setting.

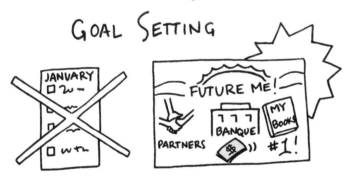

This happened during a major organizational change initiative specific to Roche's pharma group. They were stuck in a rut. No one had any idea why they were changing or what they were changing to. Subsequently, people were lethargic, unfocused, and demotivated. It was a big problem to solve. The CEO knew that a picture of the future would help. He found me, and we were a great match to tackle this problem.

To get started, we met with his leadership team and asked them to help us create a visual representation of their vision for the company's future. They drew different metaphors that we might use to represent their desired future state. This exercise pushed them out of their comfort zones since none of them thought they could draw, but their discomfort forced them to think differently and resulted in some great ideas.

Once they had chosen a metaphor they liked the best, they added elements to the picture that they wanted to see in their environment, including values, strategies, and outcomes. My team took their rough sketches and data into the studio and created a beautiful representation of their vision.

The leadership team then rolled out that vision to all managers in an all-hands offsite event that was fun and interactive. The whole event opened with the *Star Wars* theme song and the words about their challenge scrolled up in the presentation to match the opening scene in the original *Star Wars* movie. Then each functional team member outlined and spoke to the different elements in the visual. Small group discussion sessions followed, and each manager was asked to systematically roll out the vision to their employees. There were discussion cards that helped the teams understand each part of the picture and, eventually, their role in making that vision a success.

A NEW WORLD

ONCE UPON A TIME IN A COMPANY

WHERE PEOPLE WORKED HARD

TOGETHER - WAS A SMALL IDEA OF

HOW IT COULD BE BETTER - THE PEOPLE

These sessions were meant to be fun, interactive, and educational. Finally, the leadership team kept the vision picture where everyone could see it daily. They even printed it on mousepads and calendars to keep it alive and continued to refer to it in the years that followed.

Whether you are an entrepreneur, team leader, or stay-at-home dad wanting to teach your children the value of using a visual to solve a problem, here are the essential elements:

1. Reflect on your current reality—that's who you are, where you are, and what you are doing. Note what needs to change.

2. Dream of your future state—that new reality you desire.

3. Close the gap between your current and future states with three bold steps in an action plan.

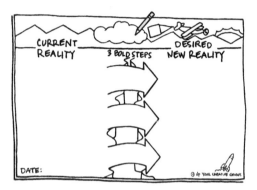

In the subsequent chapters, you will see how to use this simple Draw Your Future process as a gap analysis and goal-getting booster shot every time you need to get moving, gain clarity on what is happening, and determine your next steps.

Teams use it to set short-term actions for sprints. Entrepreneurs use it to set their vision and strategy for their business. Students use it to dream of their future careers or how they can grab that graduation cap. Families use it to help bring unity to their "home team" and help their family work on projects together.

Because it is visual, it gives you a big picture of what is happening, and that big picture will inspire you long after the drawing part is over.

2.4 Marrying Pictures with Action: Supercharging Your Image-Making Machine

In our imagination, it only takes an instant to picture ourselves in a different world—one where we live forever in a huge mansion with a buff, polished body and take endless vacations in a multimillionaire reality. However, outside our imagination, the reality is that we live in a world made of very hard matter where things happen a little more slowly due to the laws of matter and space or cause and effect.

When envisioning your future, the rush of dopamine you experience can help you act on your plan or maintain your momentum when you feel down. But you must marry that image of the future with an action plan and then do something immediately to act on it.

New Year's resolutions often fail because people tend to focus on resolving past issues or set outrageous goals like "I will go to the gym every day" when they haven't gone to the gym in a year. Goal getting sometimes takes a lot of effort, and our brain loves to tell us, "See? That was a ridiculous idea. Let's go back to the couch." The brain is geared toward negativity bias—the belief that failure is inevitable, which keeps us chained to the past.

I have found that by focusing on dreaming about the future and letting it inspire you to take small, simple actions, you will stay motivated. The image of the future, both in your brain and on paper, and the three bold steps in the Draw Your Future process are consistent activators. Bold steps are better because they can scare you out of your comfort zone. With consistent action, you can build your confidence to do the things it will take to become that desired future self. As you know, things don't just happen; you must work to make them happen.

Take each bold step and break it down into smaller actions. Then every day, do one small thing toward your future goals.

 CHAPTER SUMMARY
KEY TAKEAWAYS:

- Manifesting your future changes your actions and increases your chance of reaching your goal.

- Turning your daydreams into reality creates a dopamine-induced success high, which helps you confidently reach for new goals.

- Breaking down tasks into small actions increases your chances of success while quieting your brain's auto-negativity.

CHAPTER 3

How to Draw Your Future

First, let me introduce you to the Draw Your Future (DYF) process. Afterward, I will show you how to use it to do anything and everything. ;-)

3.1 The Draw Your Future Process: Trial and Error, Then Unbelievable Success

Get some paper and a pen and put your critic in the corner. Turn the page horizontally, and on the left side of the paper, write "current state."

On the right side, write "future state," and in the center, put three big arrows for "bold steps." I also often date the page in the corner.

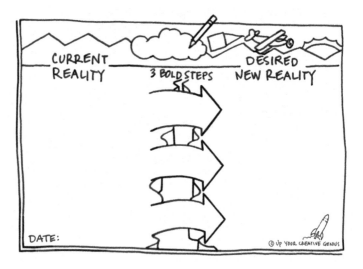

Now warm up by doodling a border all around the outside of the page.

Doodling is an instant brain integrator and releases you from the idea that these drawings need to look good. It taps into your childlike, open mindset.

I will go into how to draw at the back of this book if you want to increase your skills, but trust me, simply drawing everything you are working on will help you improve your drawing skills.

Write and capture on the left side of the page your current reality. Don't make a list—scatter everything around so you activate all parts of your brain. Capture what is going well and add a few pictures, then capture what's challenging. Keep forcing yourself to add pictures.

Your critic will not like this, so just keep reminding yourself that bad pictures are better for your memory.

Now, take a short break to stretch, draw the infinity symbol in the air, stand up, do a few jumping jacks, or drink some water. Take a few deep breaths, then sit down. On the right side of your paper under "Desired New Reality," envision your life one year (or however far you want to go out) from today in the best-case scenario. Start with what it will feel like to be you, your company, or your team in the future. The feeling is important, so grab three to four things. If the word *feeling* scares you, think of qualities and characteristics you want to experience (like abundance, success, partnership, etc.). Then add the specifics—such as the kind of partnerships you will have, the things the press will write about you or your team, the profit you will make, or even the place you will live or people you will meet, and the partners who will invest in your brilliant business ideas.

Let the desired new reality emerge organically and do not censor anything that comes through in this activity.

Once you have all the elements of your future, it's time to take some action to close that gap between these two sides of your map. Look at the current state on the left, look at the desired future on the right, and close your eyes for a second. This helps you block out all the stimulation in the room to get calm and focused. Ask yourself, "What are the three boldest things I/we can do to get from here to there?" Then as they come to you, write them down as one bold step per arrow.

3.2 Breaking It Down: Current State— What's the Problem

I have mentioned the nuts and bolts of the process for Draw Your Future above. Now, let's dive into what is happening so you can see the different aspects a little more closely.

I first realized that drawing a picture of the current state was powerful when I was facilitating a session after a bunch of people got fired in a company, and I was brought in as the change agent to talk about the process of change and help convince the team to get their butts back to work.

These people were really upset. On the day of the layoff, they had been separated into two rooms—one room for the people being fired, who were told bye-bye and go clean out your desk, and the other room for those told they were going to remain with the company. Neither group got to say goodbye to each other, and the people remaining with the company were furious.

I knew this would be a tough session, but it was incredibly difficult. Imagine spitballs and cursing all focused at me, the consultant. Immediately, my facilitation partner and I put everyone in groups and assigned them to different areas of the room. We told them to write and draw what it felt like to be them right now. After ten minutes, we brought them back together to share with us. We listened as they simply read their lists, and I captured the common themes at the front of the room on a big piece of paper.

An amazing thing happened in the very first session. As their lists were read, the people immediately started to calm down. They saw that they weren't alone in their feelings and felt validated by hearing similar feelings from others.

Whether you are working with a group or on an individual vision of the future, capturing your experience of the current reality gives you distance from it. You see the reality of where you are right in front of your face. You see patterns, old beliefs, and the truth. You say, "Oh hey, that's what I have been feeling; that's what has been happening," but it doesn't feel like "you" anymore. In this distancing technique often used in art therapy, you separate yourself from the data and the feelings. That distance helps you gain perspective and identify what is going on.

Here's a brain hack. If you find yourself really sliding down a slippery slope about the future because your left side is filled with so many challenges, try this tip.

Take your challenge and ask yourself what superpower this challenge is helping you build. That helps you shift from a victim to a growth mindset.  Do you have an image of financial stress on your map? Maybe that's teaching you to be a little more frugal. Is there a picture of fighting with your team? Maybe you are learning to improve your communication skills. This superpower activity also helps you shift over to get ready to dream of the future.

> Shift from the perspective of this is happening *to* me to this is happening *for* me.

If your critic has woken up and you aren't feeling confident about your abilities, no worries, there is one other brain hack that you can use. There is a simple, free tool called the Agilities Profiler that you can take online that will tell you your top three agilities.[7] These are the superpowers made up of your interests and strengths, which you are currently using to solve your problems. You can use them for every job in the universe. You are capable of creating any future you desire.

Now that we have our current reality on the wall, we get to step into the future . . .

3.3   Desired Future State: Future You, Unpacked

Envisioning a positive future can help your brain focus and allow your imagination to daydream with intention.

We daydream 47 percent of the time, but most of the time we do it unconsciously because we are wired for it.[8] However, focused daydreaming requires energy and effort. To set yourself up for success, it's essential to remind yourself to start with positive thoughts and eliminate the use of negatives, like "not stressed." The brain doesn't distinguish between positive or negative thoughts; it only catalogs the image. That's why it's not effective to tell your children, "Don't go near the pool," because they simply hear "pool" and go grab their bathing suits!

Starting with feelings can give an experience a higher charge. By adding specifics, you can allow the future to emerge. It's important not to censor any ideas that come up, even in a team setting. Just capture them and try to create categorical groupings. Even if you're doing a business planning session, allow yourself to add anything that emerges, even if it has to do with happy families or expansive spiritual experiences.

> It's important to understand that everything in life is connected to a bigger, mysterious picture. Therefore, it's crucial to connect all parts of your life to your dreams for your future self.

By doing so, you will evolve in your state of consciousness. As you evolve, you may want to add new things, or something may come to you out of the blue. It's important to capture every piece of it because even once the process is over, you may realize that you missed something. In that case, you can always go back and add it to the map.

During a worldwide Draw Your Future session, one of my participants was an entrepreneur who introduced me to a new way of doing the process. She would draw the future state side using only black and white. As the process began to take shape in her life, and she achieved whatever that image represented, she added color to the image. One of the things she drew was a trophy. She said she didn't know what the trophy was for—she just drew one in her future. During the year, she entered an entrepreneur's pitch competition, hoping her idea would win and receive additional funding. She didn't win that day, but about six months later, she opened her mailbox, and inside was a package that held a trophy for the best new startup in the state. That trophy looked exactly like the one in her picture.

Push yourself to imagine things that might normally feel outside your reach. Draw things that you haven't a clue how they will manifest—an office on a hill, awards, a gleaming book.

Images are powerful despite how basic they may look to you because an image of the future taps your RAS, or reticular activating system. The RAS is a part of your brain that plays a key role in regulating consciousness, attention, and arousal. It helps to create a hierarchy of images, determining what is important and what should be attended to. When you create a picture of something you desire and keep looking at it, the RAS will help to constantly pull your focus to the things that will help you achieve it.

3.4   Three Bold Steps: Add Urgency and Challenge to Scare You Out of Your Rut

It's not as difficult as it may seem to bridge the gap between where you are now and where you want to be in the future. Your brain has been working on this problem long before you even started visualizing your current and desired realities.

Your brain will offer the usual advice, such as working smarter instead of harder or simply taking action. I understand that the typical response to creating an action plan is to simply add "create a plan" to the list of steps. However, having worked with thousands of companies, I know that this approach is not inspiring. It's easy to get bored and give up, returning to the comfort of your bed with Netflix and popcorn. The map you create will likely end up in the trash, and your efforts will be wasted.

The word *bold* is key. You must find three bold steps that inspire you to action, that are high-level enough to get you moving! If you hate your job in the current state and want the freedom to do what you love in the future, well QUIT YOUR JOB is probably a bold step. It would be even better if you quit right now.

Why? Then you would be on high alert, using all parts of your creative genius to figure out how to make money and support yourself and your family while doing the things that you love.

In all my years of working with teams, I have found that one bold step is scary. And it *should* scare you a little because, in this case, scary is good.

> It is awakening your creative genius and should also be big enough that you must take a bunch of actions to do it.

The second step is bold but often tactical. Create a kickass PR campaign. Right away, you realize, "Holy crap, I do need a big campaign—maybe I need to hire help, or maybe I need to create objectives for my posts, set goals, learn how to leverage AI, etc."

FROM — CONFIDENT!

TO

SCARED

The third bold step is often a mindset shift. Build your confidence and believe that you can do it. Even though these are soft-skill ideas, they can all be broken down into actions. And it is important that you feel the urgency to get going right away right now.

Those bold steps may change over time as you refine your plan; however, they should inspire you to action. Guilt won't help you achieve your future self's dreams—action will. When you feel panicked about the future, the best thing you can do is *go do something to get there!*

Bold steps are more than rearranging your filing cabinet—they should scare and inspire you. Bold steps often are:

1. Scary and big
2. Tactical
3. Mindset shifts

3.5 Ways to Seal the Deal: Find Your Support

It's important to break down your bold steps into smaller actions you can take daily to achieve your goals. In his book *The Future You*, Brian David Johnson emphasizes the importance of becoming the person who can live in that future.[9] To do this, you need to get to know your future self by interviewing them as if they were a person outside of yourself.

Additionally, you can seek out people who are already living the life you aspire to and ask them how they got there. Remember that building relationships with people who can help you step into that future is key.

Make a list of all the people who can help and support you, and then tell them about your dream. Make sure you tell people who are there to lift you up, not tear you down, or you will find yourself back on the couch with those chips and a Netflix series.

First, identify each of your bold steps and imagine what the result will be once you have completed them. Write down all the specifics of your envisioned outcome in your journal, even if it's already on your future map.

Next, ask yourself what actions you will be taking when you are halfway there, and what actions you will be doing when you are partway there.

Finally, determine what actions you need to take right now—today. Even if it's a simple action, write it down, do it, and check it off.

It is important to act on your goals every day. Once you have completed a task, take a moment to acknowledge it and celebrate your progress. You can even raise your glass and drink something to mark the occasion. Your brain is wired to seek completion and reward, so use this to your advantage by continuously working toward your future self and enjoying the dopamine hit that comes with each accomplishment.

3.6 What Successful Draw Your Future Mappers Do: Shift Your Limiting Beliefs

Many people have tried creating a vision board before, but what makes drawing your vision more powerful than using cutouts from magazines is *you*. You are the one who draws the picture and creates the memory. The somatic experience helps you lock in the dream you hold.

Everyone has dreams for a positive future, but many people get stuck because they don't believe they can achieve them. These limiting beliefs have been with us since we were young, and there's no better time than *now* to overcome them. You have to train yourself to override your typical responses, such as "I'm not good enough" or "I'm not smart enough." No one can do it for you, so identify the old tapes you are running and replace them with positive affirmations. Seem trite? Well, it works. Don't take my word for it. Try it yourself.

Spend a little time unraveling where you formed the belief, then find a positive belief you can use to replace it. "I am smart." "I am loveable." "I can do anything."

Pay attention to what triggers your limiting beliefs, and when they start to emerge, stop the action and yell out loud or inside your head, "Change!" Then, as ridiculous as it may seem, replace and repeat those positive beliefs. For example, I make myself do it out loud . . . in public. Yep, weird but highly effective.

Then, celebrate and notice every single time you demonstrate the new belief. This signals your brain: "That's it, that's what we are going for!"

You are not your brain; you have a brain. You are a beautiful essence and fantastical spark of light and sound, swirling around and having experiences to help you grow. Remember that—because knowing that matters. And *you* matter. Enough pep talk. It's time to get to work!

Put that map somewhere you can see it every single day. Daydream it in full, living color. Imagine all the luscious experiences you have depicted on that future state side of your drawing. Then, with all that serotonin in your body, go do something to move you toward that dream.

Every week, make an action plan for that map. It may not seem like much when something small happens, but you and I both know that it is the small things over time that create that new reality. Your elbow grease and belief help you sustain the motivation to change your future, so get busy!

CHAPTER SUMMARY
KEY TAKEAWAYS:

- Draw your future self in three stages: current state, future state, and three bold steps. The more doodles, the better, and let all dreams come to life on the page.

- Distancing yourself from your current reality creates space to let go of emotions and old habits that may hold you back from change. Embrace a positive mind shift.

- Look at the map you've created, daydream about your future self, and act. Don't give your limiting beliefs time to catch up and hold you back.

PART TWO

Explain Anything Using Pictures

CHAPTER 4

How to See
Things Better

Think of the most incredible presentations you have ever experienced. What were you doing? Was it playful? Was fun an essential part? If you sat in a meeting last year but can't remember what it was about, that's probably why—it wasn't fun or visual enough.

The best offsite experiences include interactive and visual games, leaving your head filled with artifacts. These pictures help you remember what was said, what strategies were developed, and what was agreed upon during your time together. This "game-storming" starts with your imagination as you brainstorm. Weirdly enough, teams often start this process with fear-storming. Any time you start to worry, you might be heading into a fear storm, so this chapter is about how to set everybody (including you) up for success. Mindset matters. You set the stage for a positive experience, even if the problem is extraordinarily difficult.

4.1   Make It Visible and Interactive: Structure, Setting, and Materials

A powerful brainstorming session starts with your setup. The
agenda that's sent out
should be fun, visual,
and engaging. It might
be a short video enticing
people to attend, with
cartoons illustrating
how "Meetings from the
past" looked versus
"Meetings in our
FUTURE!"

> Your tone for positive outcomes
> utilizing their creative genius
> matters, so set the tone for a
> powerful experience.

Include taking the time to get into the right mindset early on
in your planning process. Set your intent to make this meeting
matter and write it down, adding a visual picture to lock it into
your hippocampus.

Next, bring materials to the session that heighten participant engagement—Post-it Notes, squish toys, noise makers, chocolate, and coffee. Take the time to consciously set these tools out on the tables in a way that feels enticing.

Arrange the seating and tables to maximize your working surface. Face the drawing or posting wall where you will be working. Set it close enough that people can see  what you are drawing, but not so close that you can't move around without them staring at your backside. LOL.

Set the tables for no more than five people; three is an even better number—it's a creative number. All good jokes have three beats to them—and good ideas too.

A good room setup will build your confidence, and your team or client will feel confident in you. A clear and compelling space tells everyone that "We are destined for greatness!"

4.2 Cheater Ways to Stardom: Catch Their Attention

Your inner critic is going to be big and loud when you are new to drawing in a meeting, so find a way to get yourself grounded. I prepopulate a very large visual agenda—one that doesn't have any words but visually depicts in images what is going to happen during our time together. People have been trained to expect PowerPoint, so surprise them with old-school visuals.

Your visual agenda doesn't need to include time stamps, which gives you wiggle room if you get behind or ahead. However, illustrate the break times and lunch for an all-day session. These are essential, and no matter your drawing skills, they will be recognizable!

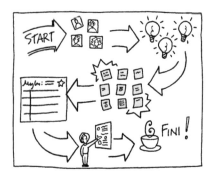

When kicking off a sales pitch or team session, introduce drawing right from the start. Use your introductions as a platform for teaching your audience drawing basics, and then ask them to draw something to represent themselves or their particular style. I show the basics first and then ask everyone to join me as I draw a square, triangle, or circle. I might even show them how to draw a simple person, starting with their hair.

Then I ask them to draw their favorite lunch or burger, add their secret sauce to it—their superpower—and share it with their table (or the room). This is another tactic to build rapport, and by introducing drawing, we are accessing all parts of the brain.

I might ask: "If you were a kitchen appliance, which would you be? Now draw that appliance in a picture to introduce yourself."

This drawing activity is a litmus test to see who they are and what they are willing to do. Most people still think drawing is for children. Therefore, you are simply tricking them into accessing their childlike state, which is the doorway to more creative ideas.

Tell participants the why behind drawing. As they draw, speak to the neuroscience behind why visuals matter. Explain that drawing integrates all parts of the brain and that visuals, even badly drawn ones, will be remembered better. If you are specifically using the Draw Your Future (DYF) process in the session, share data from "future you" studies, mentioning famous people and how they used vision boards to create reality—Oprah, Kerry Washington—you can find this information online.

Did you know that one out of five entrepreneurs use vision boards, and of those that do, 78 percent achieve their vision within three years? Build their buy-in and enthusiasm for what's to come.

All of this is helping to set you and your audience up for success using pictures to problem solve. Any warm-up tactic that involves visuals, drawing, or choosing images for self-description or what is about to happen in the session will help fuel the fire of brainstorming.

4.3 Conscious Inclusivity: It's Not about You, It's about Us

In the last decade, we have watched as people have become open to inclusion and then started to close it back down. Be a leader in this space. One perspective or viewpoint is never enough to help you find the best solution to a problem. Multiple perspectives help us think better, build better, and be better as people. As the leader of the session, set some ground rules or guiding principles to open the door for new ideas to emerge.

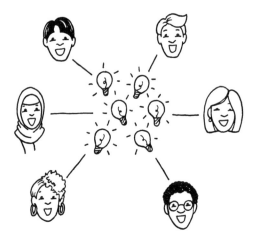

For example, when one group starts to dominate the conversation, without shaming anyone, simply remind the group to invite those who haven't been heard to participate. You are there to model the way for others and remove barriers for everyone in your session.

You can also demonstrate inclusion by what you choose to draw. Each drawing you create should include all kinds of people with different shapes, shades, sizes, and abilities.

Set the tone for collaboration, listening, and curiosity. Make space for dissenting ideas and deep discussions, and ask for visual representations of all possible solutions. Create a template with multiple doors and invite participants to label and enter each one to find new ways to solve the challenges, to sell more, to build more.

4.4 Brainstorming Tools: Mind-Mapping Solutions

Mind maps have been around since the start of visual thinking. They are a visual tool used for organizing, understanding, expanding, and presenting information, ideas, and concepts. They help you generate, organize, and structure your thinking so you can discover new ideas and relationships.

A typical mind map contains lines and words, but a visual mind map is filled with pictures and drawings of the expanded ideas. First, draw your central idea or concept in the center of your drawing space. Then create branches with different elements or subtopics of this central idea. Use as many images as you can think of on each branch. Give the teams flip-chart paper and have them use both words and pictures. Visuals allow you to see the deeper relationships between the branches and make new connections.

AI says, "Mind-mapping can be used for a variety of purposes, including brainstorming, problem-solving, note-taking, project planning, and organizing information." But what AI won't tell you is this tool is a portal to your inner superpower—your visual iconography, complete with innate linkages that your brain is housing based on everything you have ever seen, heard, watched in a movie, or read in a book or online format. While using a visual mind map, you literally tap your own internal AI functionality. The trick is to not get in its way by worrying about how good the pictures look. ;-)

Here's a simple example of a nonprofit wanting to provide eye exams and glasses in remote parts of Africa.

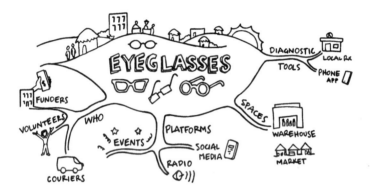

Now you try. Take a problem you want to solve and put it in the center of the picture. Then create branches of different possible solutions, and keep branching until you have exhausted the idea. Then move to a new branch. If you are selling a product, put the product in the center and surround it with all the ways it can help solve your client's issues.

The secret to unlocking new ideas, helping clients see the value in what you have to offer, or galvanizing your team's strategy is one picture away.

When you give your team a challenge to visually explore—any part of a strategy, product development, or process—they will explode with possibilities because the brain is an image-making machine.

Once you tap into that capacity, the hardest part may be funneling their ideas down to the one or two that will give you the most bang for your buck in resources and time. Be prepared with a process to manage that.

4.5 Allegories and Analogies: Giving Your Explanation a Metaphor

---

An allegory is commonly used in writing to convey a deeper meaning or message through symbols. When using illustrations in a meeting or sales pitch, an allegory helps you frame what you are working on. Perhaps you want to help your team discuss their culture, values, or purpose.

You can see here that we have a house representing the various rooms—the ground floor equals what we stand on. In this image, we filled it with furniture to represent what this team wanted their culture to be made of.

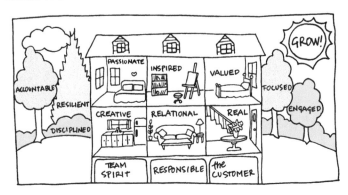

An ocean of fish is another great analogy for exploring your competition, staging a project, or the process of acquisition. Who are the big fish that are chasing you? Or that you are chasing? What is on the ocean or river's bottom that are obstacles? Or champions who will help you keep pace with the changing tide?

Your turn . . . food could be a representation of _____ (fill in the blank).

You see how this goes, and it gives your team a visual to link their ideas to their memory.

Analogies are also incredibly helpful in visual capture. They can be metaphors or similes for what the team is discussing or seeking to find. When you listen to people describing the problem, they will automatically use metaphors to illustrate their point. "We need something to help this idea get off the ground." "That's just putting fuel on the fire." People use analogies constantly, comparing or contrasting one thing to another.

> Your job, as the person running the meeting, is to listen for the visual language used to describe the situation, product, or customer and translate that into a visual metaphor.

For example, "We need this product launch to blast off" might result in you drawing a picture of a rocket with the product name on the side of the rocket ship. That "fuel on the fire" could be a stack of wood labeled with the issues.

Finding and drawing concepts using the metaphors from the dialogue will help people feel seen, heard, and truly represented. These analogous images help clarify difficult concepts, communicate intentions, and make ideas more accessible to a wider audience. If you feel the room is less engaged, ask them for ideas for the metaphor. The most powerful sessions are the ones where someone grabs the pen and starts sketching on your drawing.

Here are some examples of analogies that are commonly used in visual representation. The visual helps you solve problems because the images link you to new solutions based on your prefrontal cortex's ability to solve with pictures. The visual unlocks your memories from your hippocampus and inspires the team to dig deeper to uncover new and different ways to resolve issues.

I have drawn hundreds of mountain scenes with mountain climbers scaling new heights. It is one of the most popular metaphors in a session, which is why the Draw Your Future map has mountains on the top of the image.

Mountains can represent many things, from values to strategies or challenges to goals. Mountains are just waiting for you to scale and conquer. Their landscape can be filled with boulders or chasms. You can use a zip line to represent a shortcut or add a base camp to represent your team's preparation or training before you climb. Analogies and metaphors open the doorway to endless possibilities.

A burger is another fun image. Asking the team to describe and draw what's on their burger will help them overcome the current issues they are facing.

Drawing hack: To help you overcome the fear of drawing images on the fly, lay out your image ideas in pencil in advance. Once you know what your agenda and possible metaphor might be, sketch it out in a small version first. Then, transfer it to your bigger paper. Practice and preparation are your best offensive strategies.

> Once you realize the value of using analogies, allegories, and metaphors to capture the essence of the conversation and turn it into something memorable, you will never use traditional methods again.

The metaphors become your new memory hack. That is your task—make your session both useful and memorable.

> You are not expected to be an
> artist; you are a visual thinker,
> which is of far greater value
> to a group holding a strategy,
> product development, sales, or
> brainstorming meeting.

4.6 Road Maps: Taking Ideas from Start to Finish When Describing Your Journey

A visual road map is one of the simplest metaphors to use to build a map of your future. You can include in the drawing key milestones, timelines, and objectives of whatever you or your team are working on, be it a project, product, strategy, or implementation of a process.

A road map visual helps paint a picture and communicate the plan. It is a simple, effective, interactive tool to assist your participants in determining what obstacles they might face and what road signs, fuel, and pitstops they can leverage to achieve goals.

Building that road map will help you identify any dependencies between different elements of the project or crossroads you might come to. It often includes information about resources, budget, and any risks or challenges that could be encountered. The road map visuals might include potholes, strategy arrows, success measures in mileage, end goals in finish line flags, and deadlines in destination points.

The whole point of creating any kind of road map is to help everyone understand the plan and know the part they play in making that plan successful. It gives you a means to track progress, overcome roadblocks, and adjust as needed to ensure the project stays on track.

While you may have used spreadsheets or project management software in the past, there is nothing quite like having a picture of Dorothy on a map with the yellow brick road and letting your team move along that road together and pass the milestones needed to achieve the end goals.

In one amazing offsite, I watched a CIO play Dorothy in a skit designed to celebrate the achievements of launching a new printer product line. As he moved along the road with his team of a lion, scarecrow, and tin man, he spoke to all of the challenges that lay ahead on their way to Oz (the project name). People loved it—the yellow brick road metaphor leveled up the hilarity and fun factor in what would be a lengthy process that required consistent, dedicated teamwork. In this case, they had an interactive road map where they moved a cut out of Dorothy down the road map as the project progressed.

Creating a road map is simple. Start on the left side of the page (unless you are in a country that depicts strategy from right to left). Put the topic at the top, put a sun on the top right, and in that sun, write your end goal. Then, from left to right, start building out the strategies you will use to get there. Identify the challenges and draw those detours, roadblocks, or potholes along the way. Add stakeholders and key resources you'll need at each step.

Your end product might be messy, but once you have all the elements in place, take a picture. You can transfer any sticky notes into visuals or put the visuals into your project plan. Keep this visual up in a public place so you can see, work with, and refer to its elements often. The visual makes it easier to track where you are, make improvements along the way, and keep your brain focused on solutions.

CHAPTER SUMMARY
KEY TAKEAWAYS:

- Heighten engagement during your sessions with old-school presentations, interactive materials, and fun drawing prompts to promote the best ideas.

- Listen for metaphors that your team uses while completing the exercise and use them to capture content for the end-goal visualization.

- Utilize road maps as a memorable and interactive project management tool for your team.

Using Pictures to Unpack and Evolve Anything

CHAPTER 5

Ouch, That Challenge Hurts: Leverage It to Set the Stage to Win

If you had access to my inbox over the past twenty years, you would see countless thank-you notes from people who have used the Draw Your Future (DYF) process to make change happen. Whether selling a product to a client or starting a business, this tool is pure genius when it comes to selling anyone, including yourself, a new vision for reality.

From CEOs to children in classrooms, people wrote thank-you messages that often expressed surprise at the positive outcomes. The main message I want to communicate to you here is that selling your idea doesn't need to be complicated or a hard sell. When you use a visual picture to show the current reality with all its pain points, it's easy to illustrate the benefits of a new reality. You can paint a picture of the pain that is so compelling that you need that future with your product or process as the catalyst, assistant, and beautifier of the new life.

Here's the best part: you don't have to be an expert in drawing to do this—anyone can do it. However, the real challenge lies in helping everyone in the room, and in life, stay focused and avoid distractions. The best way to sell them on the future is to thoroughly examine the pain so you can help them see how to leap through that fire.

5.1 DYF Superpowers: Fire Up the Brain

Drawing Your Future can help teams that are underperforming or who have been distracted by restructuring or overworking. When finding yourself stuck in a rut, it is usually because you are focusing too much on the past. Focusing on the past is a typical response when you have been working long hours fixing problems or implementing technology solutions. Most teams who have been restructured, unless they've been promoted, long for the way it used to be.

Your goal is to note the pain of the past and the current state—this will help both you and them shift into the future. When they feel the pain of where they are, it will build the readiness to get out of there! They will be totally convinced that envisioning an even more outrageous future is the best course of action. They will imagine how amazing they will be and what incredible goals they will accomplish in this future world. That focus on the future fills everyone with great chemistry and the belief that anything is possible . . . because it is.

How do you capture the pain of what they feel right now? Try using the Draw Your Future process as a gap analysis. At its core, that's what Draw Your Future is. You look at what's challenging right now before you focus on where you wish you were. This current-state data gives you everything you need to focus attention on what needs to change to get out of the rut.

Put your Draw Your Future map template up on the wall or draw it out on your whiteboard, and share an overview of what you will be doing: "We are going to look at how our _____ (your focus for the session) is going. We will start with the current reality, then shift to the desired new reality, and close the gap with three bold steps. I am going to map it out for us. Yep, I am going to draw a little. And I would like you to draw as well. I know, if you are like most humans, you think your drawing skills are terrible. Don't worry, I am going to give you a brief tutorial on how to draw, and I invite you to bring your five-year-old confidence to the drawing board."

Then, do a warm-up with the team to get them to draw. Suggest basic shapes, doodling on paper, or drawing a selfie to introduce themselves to each other.

Share the reason behind the need to draw—it integrates all parts of the brain, and research shows better ideas come from a fully engaged neocortex.

5.2   The Moment of Truth: Enter the Pain Cave

Ask them what their business, product, or team looks like right now— what's going well and what is challenging. If it's a small team, you can have them jot a few notes on Post-its first so the introverts have a chance to think before the extroverts take over. Or, if you have a large group, ask them to write notes individually and choose two or three things that are going well and two or three challenges.

Then invite them to debrief, starting with what's going well first.

> Your job is to capture what they say on the left side of your map, remembering not to make a list.

Listing taps into the analytical side of the brain, making everyone more rigid.

Scatter their words around the page and draw a few pictures. Remember, if you are doing this for the first time, you will be slow to draw, so just know that when you take a break, you can go back and fill in your map with pictures or color.

Most groups tend to start with what is going poorly, so if they start listing the challenges, make sure to write them in red marker. To help them feel the pain, remember that red is your pain marker. Then use a light blue marker for good things. Now, you should have a picture of what they feel good about and what they are struggling with.

5.3 Blind-Spot Mitigation: Getting Under the Problem

When you draw in red on the left side of the picture, that is all your group will remember—*the problems that need solving*. This is fantastic for selling your ideas or product, but if you are running this process with your team, they can slide down into "woe is me," and the next thing you know, people will start

finger-pointing. In a team situation, state the obvious: the way your brain works is that it is a problem-solving machine, so it will try solving these things right now.

There is always something under the challenges, so if you have the time, look at some of the blind spots you see to better understand them. You want to know what they are getting out of this challenge or what's being learned from that particular blind spot. The goal is to help them identify the warning signs so they know what to do when they show up again.

Using the visual, transfer the challenges to a separate area, then ask the room to help you identify the blind spots. Ask, "What are we currently doing?" or "What do we say to ourselves that creates a blind spot to an opportunity?"

For example, some people feel like they know it all, so they don't need to hire anybody to help. Others worry they don't have any money to hire people. Subsequently, they spend energy doing small things to distract themselves or try to fix 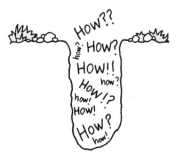 the little stuff when they should be looking at the bigger picture.

Some teams feel they need more research, so they never get going. They just keep staying in the "how hole" and don't move forward with the project or product. Or they might feel that everything has to be perfect.

These are some of the blind spots. Capture as many blind spots as they surface and choose one that is the most prominent, then write it on a big piece of paper or in a separate area.

Next, do a visual cost/benefit analysis for that blind spot. What's the cost in terms of time, money, energy, and people that might be impacted by continuing to have this blind spot?

Figure out what it's costing you, and then shift over to what the benefits are. Meaning, what's the gift of that blind spot? What's it giving? What are you learning from it? What insights are you getting from it?

As you look at the costs in that area, figure out what superpower this blind spot is helping you develop. Because when we shift from feeling victimized by our blind spots, we shift into a place of power, and in that power is our new superpower. We learn how to hire people better, invest better, or let go of things and let other people take charge.

The team will suddenly realize the reason they need to deal with the blind spot and, with the new information the visual has given them, can choose a course of action to do something about it.

5.4 Future Casting: Relieve the Pain and Sell the Future

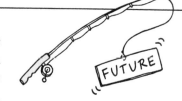

Okay, suddenly it feels like enough pain already! Your team is ready to move on. You'll be able to tell because they will automatically start talking about the future. To get everyone ready and access all their creative genius, you must unhitch their wagons from the past and the problems they have been focusing on.

Start by doing a brain gym activity to warm up and shift their energy and brain focus. A simple brain gym activity is to tap the right elbow on the left knee and then reverse the action, tapping the left elbow on the right knee. You can also ask them to do jumping jacks or take a deep breath. It's helpful to get them to move around and drink a sip of water or coffee. These activities shift their brains' focus so they can be more open.

Future casting is the essential ingredient to winning work while captivating the room. Imagination is the key to effective future casting. It is the innate talent that everyone is born with. It's one part of the brain that is automated to help you problem solve to get yourself in and out of any conundrum that you might encounter.

If you don't pay attention to building your imagination by drawing, reading, brainstorming, or playing, your brain will default to its negativity bias, which is its natural state.

The negativity bias exists because when we were cave people, we had to run away from the dinosaur before we got eaten. Or we had to figure out a way to make fire before, "Oh no, they're going to eat our dinner!" Negativity bias is its natural default.

Do everything you can to shift the attention from negative thinking to optimize the creative, resourceful part of the brain.

The imagination has an active neural workspace, and when you put yourself in the play space of your imagination, you can solve anything.

Your imagination is linked to your reticular activating system (RAS). When you put something into the play space that you want and keep playing around it, everywhere you look in your life, you will begin to see what you're playing with in here (in your imagination), out there.

Imagination is also a predictor of the future. If you spend all your time thinking about the negative things that could happen, guess what? The RAS is going to pull all that to you. Subsequently, like *Groundhog Day*, you'll experience that thing you don't want again and again and again and again.

It's time to take charge and use the prefrontal cortex part of your brain to problem solve for things that have a positive feeling or outcome.

The easiest way to create an expansive mindset is by asking a question. Any kind of question you ask is going to put you into that play space, where you can mix and match images from your hippocampus to dream up all you want to see in your future environment.

Your goal is to draw pictures of what you see in your imagination. When you combine a question with a drawing of the future, it builds new neural pathways.

5.5 Future Casting with a Focal Point to Discover the Unusual Solution

To future cast with a focal point, first, choose a part of the future that intrigues your client to use for this activity. Here are three different ways of accessing new information about it using future casting.

1.   Look at the element of the future and ask the group, "What will achieving this teach me?" Take some time to reflect and capture some notes. Now, have them brainstorm an exhaustive list of possible things to do to put this element in place in the future. Try to come up with at least forty things that could be done in the next three weeks. Make them crazy and outrageous, and make the method used to achieve them challenging.

Examples might be simply finding a workaround or doing something that could get someone fired. The actions might be things that they always thought would be the most fun and playful way to do business. Your task is to inspire creativity. Get everyone to really go crazy.

2. Take that exhaustive list and have your participants choose three of the most provocative ideas—provocative meaning the most scary or crazy and what they perceive as game changers. Write those three down, and either you or someone from the team should draw a simple icon to represent each one. Now, invite them to give each idea a plausibility score.

On a scale of one to five, how plausible are they? Could they really happen? One being no, probably not, and five being wow, this idea has potential!

3. Reflect on the scores and imagine using the best idea. Now, draw a picture of this team at the finish line, having used this provocative idea to get there.

5.6   Future Casting Using Randomity and Third-Person Interpretation

Here's another super fun way to get a deeper understanding of the potential future. Focus on one element of the desired future and ask what we need to know more about to step into that future element.

If you are in a room with books, invite the group to walk to the bookshelf and count out to the seventh book, pull it down, and open it to a paragraph. Don't censor what you get. If it's a blank page, all right, that's what you'll be using. If it has a quote there, just write it down.

If you are in a digital environment, use something like ChatGPT or any AI tool to do this. Let's say you are an education leader, and the element you have chosen for this activity is a new partner for funding. Ask the group to pose a question to the AI tool, giving it a role. A prompt might be: "Take on the role of a nonprofit leader in education and come up with seven ideas for partnerships with a potential funder." Use the seventh suggestion that AI gives you for this activity.

Then you will create an imaginary interpreter to help you understand the AI-generated content you have received. They are the "third person." You are person number one, the book or AI answer is the second person, and the third person is the interpreter. This is like a Magic 8 Ball. It's going to give you advice using that passage.

On a separate piece of paper, write a question that you want to ask the interpreter. Your question might be, "What do you have to tell me about this future element?" or "What growth do I need to achieve?" or "What needs to change for our team to meet those potential partners?" Then write words and draw pictures of whatever is dropping into your thinking from that passage.

What's the advice from this third person, and what's it telling you? Reflect on your pictures and come up with a plan to move forward and things you can do as a result of this random experience.

5.7   Future Casting Using Six Questions and a Writing Activity

1. FEEL
2. THINK
3. PHYSICAL SENSATION
4. ACTION
5. LEARNING
6. IMPORTANCE

The last future-casting brainstorm activity is a combination of visuals and words. Here, we're going to use a circle of questions to get in and expand our thinking to broaden our ideas of the future. We're considering six things in this, so you could use an element of the future you want more information about, like that new imagined partnership, or you might use this activity to jumpstart your bold steps.

Answer these questions:

1. How do I *feel* about this future? What do I absolutely love about this element of the future or this overarching future? Draw a picture of what it feels like.

2. What do I *think* about it? What's going on in my head about it? What beliefs do I have about it? What am I thinking about? Draw a picture of what you think about it.

3. What *physical sensations* am I experiencing when I think about this future? Draw a picture of the physical sensations you are having.

4. What *actions* could I take on this right away to make it happen? Draw pictures for each action you could take.

5. What am I *learning* about in the process of dreaming this future? Draw your key learnings.

6. *Why* is this *element* of the future *important*? Draw a big question mark and add to it all of your thoughts about why this element is critical.

Reflect on these pictures and your answers.

The point is not to come up with big solutions but to ask a series of holistic questions to dig in and unpack the future using our imagination.

5.8   Putting It All Together

Take everything that you've drawn, all of the sketches, scribbles, and notes from the examination of this one element of your future or the overarching future. Then ask yourself, what are the key takeaways from these activities? Is there a new direction I need to take or something new I hadn't thought about that's important to this future?

Take time to look at the specifics—what partnerships do you have, or what products have you created? If you are working with a team, ask them to call these out to you and capture them on your map. You can slow the pace of this to your writing capabilities. If you have a big group of introverts, let them write one insight per post and bring them to the front of the room. You can put those right on the map and then transfer them in your handwriting as you have time.

Ask the team to add some specifics for what they will see in the future. By adding more detail to the image, they will create a stronger bond to their future selves.

That's how we make change more easily—we bond with the future and tap into our RAS.

As you continue to add to the image, it will start to come together organically. The tenor of the room will change dramatically—people will get loud, laugh, and smile. This is from tapping into the oxytocin from drawing, digging in, and dreaming about the future.

Note: If you are *not* getting a positive response, be curious. Is there an elephant in the room? Why do they seem stuck? Do not try to continue without addressing it. Ask them what's getting in their way, and then listen. You may have to stop the activity and go back to blind-spot mitigation. However, with most groups, I have found that just listening will help them to shift.

If you are selling your services in this session, this section is powerful for your client. When seeing the future emerge in real time, people become super inspired to get there. The key to closing a deal using this process is to point out how powerful that future is and how you can help them to achieve it.

This is the high point; now we must move into the rolling-up-our-sleeves part—the three bold steps.

CHAPTER SUMMARY

KEY TAKEAWAYS:

- Take charge of your prefrontal cortex by creating new neural pathways, daydreaming your future and drawing pictures to bring them to life, while silencing your repetitive negative thoughts.

- Utilize AI as a "third person" idea generator when brainstorming ideas to solve problems.

- Stretch your imagination with future casting by asking yourself questions that help you understand that future element better.

CHAPTER 6

Three Bold Steps: Closing the Gap with Your Solution to Win the Day

To make change, you must feel the pain of the present and the pull toward the future. Both things will fuel your willingness and urgency to make change happen—to *do* something about it.

When I was first developing the Draw Your Future (DYF) process, I was trying to sell my services as a graphic recorder. I would run a rough version of the process with a prospective client. In those days, "visual thinker" wasn't even a thing. No one had any drawings in their offices of their vision, so it was often an uphill battle to get them to see the value of having a picture of their strategy. I would feverishly draw a picture of how their company or team was going now, the future, and then how they could close the gaps. They would nod and talk and watch, and all the while, I was thinking, "Yes! They are going to hire us!" Then I would talk about a follow-up session with their leadership team, and BOOM—the door would slam shut.

But they always wanted me to leave the picture. They'd just gotten a free consulting session, and they knew it!

If you are selling your services, this is the part where you ask the potential client to look at the left side of the page (their current state), look at the right side (their future state), and then emphasize how your services can help them close the gap. You might build up the fact that people often are afraid to step into the future and that's why you are there—the expert to help them bridge the gap. When you watch any Instagram sales video today, you will see this process in most pitches.

6.1 Better Together: The Secret Selling Sauce

When you are with a group or team, the time for leveraging their thinking power is during the three bold steps. If you have used the DYF tool, you already have a current reality and have envisioned the desired future reality.

Now you just need to close the gap. If I want them, as a group, to come up with the solutions, I invite everyone to look at the current state, then look at the desired future state, and *then* close their eyes and ask their creative genius—that part that has seen, watched, heard, and dreamed solutions of all kinds—to help identify the three boldest things they can do to close the gap.

It's important to explain that making those steps *bold* will get them out of the rut of doing what they have always done. Earlier, in chapter 3, we discussed the pattern in the bold steps. Often, the first bold step is truly bold, like "quit my job" or "launch my business." It's something that stirs up a little fear. That's when you know you have settled on something that truly needs to happen— it scares you a little.

The second bold step might be bold, but it's also tactical, like "build a marketing plan" or "hire a team." It sometimes supports the first bold step, but not always. It can be a stand-alone step related to a part of your life that has required cleaning up for a while. If it feels familiar to you, like you've tried it before, then up the ante on it. Make it a little bolder so you can feel a difference in the phrasing of it.

The third bold step is often a mindset shift. To make change in our lives, we need to shift the way we think and step into a new way of thinking that will help us believe it's possible. This step is often something like "believe we can," "be courageous," or "100 percent me 24/7."

My clients came up with the above examples to solve their own problems. But if you came to sell your product, this is your time to invite potential clients to imagine what you could do together. Take each bold step and leverage your expertise to shape the strategy you would use to help them cross over the gap and into the future. Show them that you are better together.

If you use any of the imagination-expanding future-casting activities, there will be many ideas to use to close the gap. Remember that your job is to elevate those ideas to the most strategic level. This highest level means you will have to do maybe five to ten things before that comes to be—before you can cross the bridge and manifest that desired new reality.

If you are a project manager, here's your opportunity to share the ways you can help the team implement their solutions. Without giving everything away, you can outline which parts of the potential strategy might be tricky. All the while, you're drawing this out, digging in to see which pathway they need. While you might love this piece of work, perhaps the contacts you have can better help them. I have found that the less attached I am to whether they hire me and the more focused I am on what they really need, the more often I am hired to help. By letting go of your agenda, you'll demonstrate how to be better together.

6.2   Action Planning

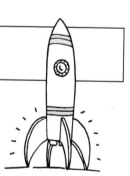

The bold steps are the fins on the rocket ship, and each needs to be broken down into small actions to start blasting on today.

Put these actions into your calendar, and then, as a team or individual, get busy. I often choose one thing to do right away from each of my lists and go and do it before I get sidetracked by social media.

Every day, your goal is to look at that map or have your team look at that map and take in the vision. Choose one thing from the vision, close your eyes, and double-click on it—daydreaming as if this element were happening right now. Play out the vision of the future, discover what's underneath it, and build it out. Be sure to have a pen and paper handy to take notes on what you observe. Add how you feel, what is happening around you, and who is in your picture of the future. Look, absorb, get inspired, then go do something to make it happen. Right away.

The most important thing to remember is that your brain is trainable. And it is trained through rewards. It is a pattern-making machine that loves to complete a cycle of anything—positive or negative.

Your goal is to help it complete a thought, activity, or action by initiating something and then completing it—as small as it may seem.

Here's another trick: When you complete anything, whether it's making a list, calling a contact, writing a page of your book, or having a team meeting, always celebrate success—no matter how small. Raise your coffee cup and declare, "I drink this coffee in celebration of completing _____."

Set a goal, take action, and celebrate each small step.

6.3   Lasting Solutions: Pictures

Here are key things that people who have used the Draw Your Future process most successfully have shared with me.

TIP 1   REGULARLY REVIEW YOUR DRAWING TO KEEP YOUR VISION ALIVE

Set aside time regularly to revisit and review your visual representation of the future. This reinforces the goals in your mind and helps you stay connected to your vision. You can also add to your drawing or color the images in the future as they happen.

TIP 2 BREAK DOWN YOUR VISION OR ADJUST YOUR BOLD STEPS TO ACHIEVING IT

Once a bold step has happened, or if it no longer feels relevant, create a new one.

TIP 3 MAKE SURE YOU HAVE BUILT A PLAN WITH SMALL, ACHIEVABLE ACTIONS

Get more detailed about your actions by creating a road map that outlines the specific tasks needed to achieve each part of your vision.

TIP 4 SET SHORT-TERM GOALS EACH WEEK THAT ALIGN WITH YOUR OVERALL VISION

Achieving these smaller goals provides a sense of accomplishment and keeps you motivated.

TIP 5 REMEMBER TO PUT YOUR MAP SOMEWHERE YOU CAN SEE IT EVERY DAY

Surround yourself with visual reminders of your vision. This could be a printed copy of your drawing, digital wallpapers, or even a tattoo. These reminders serve as constant reinforcement.

TIP 6 REGULARLY ASSESS AND CELEBRATE YOUR PROGRESS

Take time each week to review how you have done on your action steps. Evaluate your progress, celebrate achievements, learn from any setbacks, and adjust your plan as needed.

TIP 7 **SHARE YOUR VISION WITH OTHERS**

Communicate your vision with friends, family, or a mentor *who you know will support* your vision.

> Sharing your goals makes you more accountable and opens the door for valuable feedback and support.

TIP 8 **STAY FLEXIBLE AND OPEN TO ADAPTING YOUR VISION BASED ON NEW INFORMATION OR CHANGING CIRCUMSTANCES**

Flexibility is key to overcoming unexpected challenges and finding alternate routes through the obstacles you will encounter.

TIP 9 **DEVELOP NEW HABITS THAT ARE ALIGNED WITH FUTURE YOU**

Consistent, positive actions create a routine that reinforces your commitment to your goals.

TIP 10 ENVISION YOUR SUCCESS BY TAKING TIME EACH DAY TO MENTALLY PICTURE YOURSELF ACHIEVING YOUR GOALS

Visualization can enhance motivation and keep your vision at the forefront of your mind.

TIP 11 STAY POSITIVE AND PERSISTENT

Rome wasn't built in a day. Maintain a positive mindset even when facing obstacles. Persistence is often the key to overcoming challenges and making progress.

Remember, drawing your future is just the beginning. The real work lies in consistently taking steps toward your vision and adapting as needed along the way. You've got this! You can do it!

CHAPTER SUMMARY
KEY TAKEAWAYS:

- Revisit your future drawing often to help keep your goals at the forefront of your mind.
- Adjust your bold steps and consistently review your progress to increase your chance of success. Break down tasks into small, less intimidating steps.
- Celebrate every little thing and envision your success to fuel motivation.

.

PART FOUR

If Your Drawing Skills Suck: How to Become a Human Highlighter

CHAPTER 7

Just Start Doodling

Ninety-eight percent of the people I meet or who have watched my "Draw Your Future" (DYF) TEDx Talk say, "My drawing skills suck." And for most of us, this is true, not because you can't draw but because you haven't practiced drawing.

When I first saw someone draw a picture in a meeting, I was fascinated by the impact it had on me and my colleagues. We were mesmerized, and I remember thinking, "I want to do that—it looks so fun."

Immediately, I found someone who needed a graphic recorder to capture meeting notes on flip charts. On the borders of the pages, I drew little images—very, very basic stuff. People went crazy; they loved the flip charts so much that they asked if they could keep them.

You will be shocked by how much people like seeing the most basic of drawings in your in-person or online meetings. The pictures remind everyone that their words matter and that the meeting can be fun!

I was not a trained artist when I started. I taught myself to draw, which is why, to this day, I have to laugh when people say, "You are such an amazing artist." LOL, right! You can learn to draw. I have trained hundreds of people through online and in-person classes. Each person walks out of one session with a keen sense of the drawing style. If you stick with it, meaning you just doodle every day, you inevitably get better. Practice makes perfect. Get your pen, and let's get started.

7.1 BASICS of DRAWING
Fast-Track Your Drawing

Basic shapes make up the world. A square, a triangle, a circle, a comma, a period, or a line. Everything is made of these shapes. Just look around to see.

Draw a square. Now, write some 7s in that square and turn it into a building.

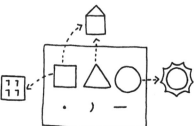

Put some mountains behind it.

Turn a circle into your favorite emoji.

Look at the images you drew and say out loud (and loudly), "That is fantastic!" You must rewire your brain to keep your critic at bay. I recommend you do that every time you draw. Boom, you just hit the success button, and a dopamine delivery is on its way.

7.2 Look to See: Develop Keen Observation to Level Up Your Drawing Skills

Your imagination is feeding you images every single moment. Some are the ones you see with your eyes; others are the ones you imagine when daydreaming. Your job is to become observant of what you are seeing.

Start by looking at something in front of you with great intensity. Notice its basic shape, then where the shadow falls behind or beside it. Now, recreate that object and its shadow. This is how you start getting better—by looking at something and then recreating it on paper.

We see so many images every single moment that our brain can't possibly process each one, or it will implode. Naturally, it sifts out the images you have seen many times and deletes the details of them. Your job is to look at those details. What does a cup look like? How is it constructed? Where is the handle placed? If you are looking down from above the cup, what do you see?

Draw it here:

What do doors look like when they are open?

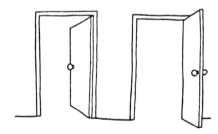

How do you draw a corner in a room?

In my early years as a consultant, I flew on airplanes almost every week. On each plane ride, I would open my journal and draw what I saw in front of me, like the aisle of seats and overhead bins. Then, to challenge myself to draw quickly, I would attempt to capture the people as they passed by me in the aisle.

In my first graphic recording internship, I learned the power of using a drop shadow. Imagine that in every picture you draw, there is a sun above you to the right that casts a shadow to the left of the image. Now, take a pencil or a gray brush-tipped marker and draw a thick gray line on the left side of the image, where that shadow would fall. This technique makes any two-dimensional object suddenly appear to be three-dimensional.

Try it here:

Practice Makes Perfect: Quick Capture—How to Sideline the Ongoing Inner Critic

The most difficult thing in learning how to draw quickly is your inner critic. In my early years, I had to constantly remind myself to override the inner voice. If I let my fear take over, I couldn't draw a single thing. I would create a whole four-by-eight-foot map full of words with only a few images.

You must force yourself to draw quickly and without censorship.

Your brain will feed you images of what to draw while you are listening to someone speaking, but your task is to synthesize what is important in what they are saying and capture that essence into an image.

This takes practice, and an easy way to start is to turn on the news and capture what's discussed. Or when you are in a meeting and don't have to participate, draw what the speaker is saying. Start by drawing the person and then title your page. Then, just doodle what they are talking about and the concepts they outline. Let it flow.

When I first learned to draw, there weren't any smartphones that I could look at to get an idea of an image. Subsequently, I would bring other people's drawings from meetings they had captured and copy ideas from their images. Initially, my brain simply couldn't work that fast. My image bank wasn't as accessible as it is now. I had to train it by feeding it images and icons.

Back to the meeting you are doodling. Listen for the essence of what is happening.

> Just as your brain sorts and sifts for the most essential things to remember, doing live capture requires you to do two things at once: listen and synthesize what you are hearing.

Then, draw or write that synthesized thought or image on the paper or tablet.

You have no room for the critic in this process, or you will stop listening to what's being said because you are listening to your critic. The way you know your critic has taken over is you will lose the speaker's train of thought. Don't worry—just snap out of it and keep going.

Over time, you will learn to silence the critic by just laughing. I still find myself laughing at something I have drawn.

Remind yourself that this is supposed to be fun, that no one knows what you "should" be drawing, and it's all up to you. Trust me, someone will tell you if you miss something important as a graphic recorder. They still do it all the time in meetings I am drawing, and I am so happy for it!

Remember, when the meeting is over, look back at your drawing, find something you really like, and say to yourself, "That is fantastic!" Because it is.

7.4 Finding the Best Drawing Materials for You

Materials make a huge difference in creating visuals. Because I go through so many materials every year, I try to use the least expensive materials I can find. Here are my favorites. (PS: I am not sponsored by these people.)

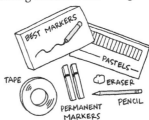

1. **Mr. Sketch markers:** You can use a chisel tip pen to write words, and it's fun to use bright colors. These markers come in a twelve-pack with enough colors to give all your lettering a pop.

2. **Black permanent marker:** This is essential for drawing images. It must be permanent, not water soluble, so you can add color to the images. A watercolor black will bleed onto your light-colored markers and be ugly on the drawing. BOO! Here are my favorite black permanent pens:

    •   **Neuland markers:** I prefer a chisel tip, but everyone has their own preference. While a Sharpie can work well, the smell gives me a headache.

    •   **Copic markers** (#100): This is a double-tipped pen—one side a chisel and the other a fine tip, which is great when you are drawing people. Plus, this is alcohol based, so you can use it on yourself if you get a cut. ;-)

3. **Tombow brush-tipped markers:** These are for coloring in the images. While you can get Crayola markers to do this, I find that Tombow dual-tipped markers last a long time. I probably still have some markers that I bought ten years ago.

4. **Drawing paper:** Purchase rolls of paper for drawing on. Most graphic recorders use a four-by-eight-foot piece of paper, so buy this paper in rolls. You can get a sixteen- or twenty-pound banner roll from art supply stores online. These come in big rolls, so you must roll off some paper so that it doesn't rip when you try to put it up on the wall.

5. **White artist tape:** I prefer the one-inch type. You should use artist tape because it won't leave residue on the wall.

6. **Retractable lightweight knife:** This is to cut your paper.

7. **Pencil and eraser:** I prefer to pencil in some ideas, images, or even the logo on my layout. Then, I write or draw over them and erase the pencil lines before I start to color.

8. **Chalk pastels and tissues:** Get a pack of twenty-four colors in the least expensive chalk pastels you can find. You will go through a lot of chalk pastels if you want to finish your picture. You'll add pastel to the image and then blend it with tissues.

Note that not all graphic recorders or visual thinkers use pastels, and you can get away with just a black pen and a few colors. You'll be surprised by the variation of styles different graphic recorders have—just

search for graphic recording on the internet. It's a good way to get new ideas.

If you store any of your colored markers lying on their side, they will last you a long time. The permanent markers are the ones that will run out. While you may have created a Draw Your Future (DYF) template in advance, you will still draw lots of images with this permanent marker, so make sure it is a fresh, new marker every time you are going to do a session.

9. **Resources for images:** Another good resource to get ideas can be found at the International Forum of Visual Practitioners (IFVP.org). You can see samples of people's work and get ideas for images, as well as find graphic recorders for hire. They also have annual conferences in different parts of the world where you can meet amazing people.

DIGITAL DRAWING

If you prefer to use a tablet, see if you can try a few before investing and practice drawing with it. There are many options—iPad, Surface, Wacom—and I'm sure many more by the time you read this.

The iPad has the application Procreate built into the tablet, so you don't have to learn to use a complicated program like Adobe Photoshop or Illustrator to get started.

Wacom makes a variety of tablets that plug into your computer, and you can use any application to draw into.

Be sure to understand all the nuances of your tablet before you start drawing for others. Practice integrating the drawing into the technology. Rehearse building the various layers so you understand how to do it easily and well. I am not an expert on digital drawing, but many are. You can easily find a tutor and get busy.

DRAW YOUR FUTURE TEMPLATE

You can download a copy of the Draw Your Future map at upyourcreativegenius.com/store/. That starts you off with everything in place, but you may want to create your own style, so be creative!

While I use a tablet for studio work, I prefer live drawing on paper. One reason is that I learned to draw that way, but I have also found that watching someone draw on paper activates the audience's curiosity. I can build the drawing, starting with black lines and maybe adding certain words using colored pens. Then I add my drop shadow, color in the images, and add pastel at the very end. This gives the illustration a "finished" look.

The visual progression of the drawing builds the audience's intrigue, anticipation, and excitement when they see their words come to life in a final image. They will often take many pictures in person or ask for a copy.

I have done both live in-the-room drawings and online sessions from my studio. For both, you will need a flat wall, and you must double the paper on that surface because your permanent marker will bleed through to the next layer. You don't want it to bleed through to the hotel or office wall.

LIGHTING

If you are in your home, be sure to have good lighting. I use five box lights for a four-by-eight-foot wall space. This way everything is illuminated evenly, and you are brightly lit as well!

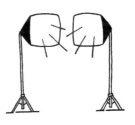

CHAPTER SUMMARY
KEY TAKEAWAYS:

- Don't be intimidated by drawing. Everyone starts from the beginning, and the base of everything is simple shapes and symbols.

- Improve your drawing skills by using keen observation and practice drawing things around you as you see them.

- Find the right materials for you, whether physical or digital, and invest in them. Good materials will last longer and perform better than budget items.

CHAPTER 8

How to Build an Inner Icon Library

The biggest hurdle you will have when going through the Draw Your Future (DYF) process is simply coming up with image ideas. It's easy to think, "Okay, what's an image for the word *idea*?" The first thing that might come to mind is a lightbulb, right? But you could also use a lightning bolt or draw an explosion in the sky around a picture of a brain. You could also draw so many, many other things. Yet when you are up at that wall or using that pencil, knowing that you must come up with an image, you might initially draw a blank.

Building an inner icon library creates an easy shortcut for your brain to the vast possibilities of things you could draw.

It just takes a little focused attention and practice. In this chapter, you'll learn how to sort and stack images so you can truly become a tagged Wizard at the Whiteboard.

8.1 Scaffold Iconography: Source Images and Draw Them to Lock Them to Memory

Images for some words are easy. *Writing* equals pen and paper or an open book. *Vision* equals a big sun with the word *vision* written on it or a person holding binoculars looking off into the distance. *Big data* equals stacks of computer gear or a big circle of whatever you think data should look like . . .

Each image that comes to you happens in a nanosecond. Retaining and choosing the image is what feels difficult at first. To help yourself get quicker, think of a recent meeting you attended. Capture all the words you think the team used most, including all the sidebars and jokes.

Make a list of these and then next to each word, draw the first thing that comes to your mind.

Here is a sample list for practice:	Now let's add more complex ones:
Agenda	Strategy
Ground rules	Inclusion
Data points	Equity
Process flow	Culture
Wins	Baseline
Challenges	Empathy
Product launch	Shortages
Timelines	Lack of staffing
Next steps	Leadership

Once you have drawn whatever drops into your mind (and don't worry if you have some blank areas . . . everyone does), use your best friend Google, Bing, ChatGPT, or whatever is currently trending, and enter the word and sort at the top for images. This resource is your new best friend.

Even today, I sometimes write the word first and then add the image after I've had a chance to sort for a cool image. I simply look it up and copy it. Copying an image idea is a totally acceptable thing to do.

Your next job is to simply practice using those icons, so you have them in your brain. Many people have asked me, in fact, begged me to create an icon book so they can flip a page and find an image. I have created icon sheets but have not found icon books easy to navigate. It's much easier and faster to navigate my phone.

Another tool I used to train myself to draw better was *The Firefly Visual Dictionary*. It's a book of illustrations with all kinds of things, from planes to saws to bugs. I would open the book randomly and find an image. I would study it first, then close my eyes and recreate it in my mind—almost as if I were communicating with it to help me understand its construction better. I would then open my eyes and draw it without looking back at the picture. Finally, I would compare my drawing to the image and add more details. This is all without getting critical. If my drawing looked different, I would laugh at it and try drawing it again. All this time, I was training myself to let go and let my own style emerge.

Build your own inner icon library and practice, practice, practice. Remember to say "That is fantastic!" because this reinforcement pays off.

Start with simple, universal icons to consolidate concepts into one picture.

One of the most common approaches to capturing notes in a meeting is to write down *everything*. But this is not going to leave you any space for anything else—like images. LOL!

A large part of the reason we seem to forget concepts and meeting content is that while our long-term memory is virtually limitless, our short-term or "working" memory has a much, much smaller capacity.

In fact, we can only remember three to five pieces of information there at any given time.[10]

Your job is to capture the essence of what is being discussed, not all the details. If you watch a graphic recorder or live performance illustrator in a session, they will wait to understand the whole paragraph of what someone is saying before capturing it in two words and an image.

I fall into the category of being a prolific graphic capture person, meaning my maps are filled with data. While I have tried to limit the number of words, I find that people want to be accurately represented, which sometimes means more words. (That could also be an excuse, but go with me here.) As a result, I trained myself to capture those words and images into a bigger image landscape, not like a long-streaming arrow, although I have drawn those, but more into a kind of nature landscape or space landscape. This serves as a placemat for the ideas to sit within. Sometimes, the image will be pulled from the client's website imagery or product types, while sometimes, I just make it up. Those are often the ones my clients like the best. But I have regular backgrounds that I use, perhaps out of habit, but mostly out of knowing when something works and reusing it. Why recreate the wheel, right?

> Finding the universal iconography that people carry in their heads about their products, challenges, or future will help to reflect their consciousness.

That's really your job—reflecting in a visual form the consciousness and content of the gathering. Practice and time will build your confidence and skills to tap into that universal thinking that is floating in the room.

8.2 Practice Makes Perfect: Hearing the Words but Listening for Pictures

When people talk, they paint you a picture. "We want to really nail those KPIs!" "This product is going to explode in the marketplace!" "I'm telling you, this is a game changer."

Look at each of those sentences and brainstorm all the metaphors that are used. For example, "nailing" could be a bunch of images hung up within your paper using nails to hang them. For "explode in the marketplace," we want to be careful not to trigger someone in the room who has had a real experience with this. But we could show a ripple effect, like a product dropping into a pond. Game changer . . . what image comes to your mind to draw?

> Listening for and drawing out
> the metaphor is one of the
> most powerful ways to reflect a
> meeting's content.

In the Draw Your Future process, we are looking at the current reality on the left, the desired new reality on the right, and the closed gap with three bold steps.

Naturally, I have developed a template to make it easier for people who feel their drawing skills are lacking. However, I always try to draw something different across the top of the map or in the background, even if I am using the same process.

Discuss with the team what that vision of the future might look like in advance so you have a few ideas to take into the room for the session. Prepping yourself with ideas and not being attached to them will save you time. *And* your anxiety will be low. Even if you never use a single idea out of the ones you planned for, you will feel prepared, and preparation will keep your pulse slow.

CHAPTER SUMMARY

KEY TAKEAWAYS:

- Start off by building an icon library in your brain that you can naturally reference anytime you draw while listening.

- Hear the words, but listen for pictures. Capturing these images will help your short-term memory summarize what's important during meetings.

- Your job is to capture the essence of what is being discussed, not all of the details.

CHAPTER 9

Getting Started: Performance Drawing for Others

The first time you draw for other people, you will be scared. Transform this fear into anticipation and excitement by being totally prepared, so you are ready and not scrambling to keep up. Have fun, laugh, and enjoy the feedback that you *will* get. Here are some simple ways to prepare yourself and your space for what's coming.

9.1 Setting Up Your Space: Organizing Materials in the Right Place for the Right Uses

One of the most important things to know before going into what Sunni Brown, author of *The Doodle Revolution*, calls "performance doodling" is knowing what the walls look like. You need a space to draw on that is at least four feet wide at your drawing height and eight feet long.

Occasionally, you might be asked to draw in a room filled with whiteboards. This is a small miracle. Most of the time, you will be in a hotel room with carpeted walls, an air wall, or a wall broken up by light sconces. It's important to know what the wall surface is made of, so ask the event coordinator to take pictures to send to you. This way, you will be prepared with the materials you need to make whatever surface you get flat, as smooth as possible, and usable.

These are the things that I have in my toolkit to help me set up my drawing space:

Packing tape: The clear kind that you pack boxes with. This will cover a seam in an air wall and make it a flatter surface.

T-pins: These are for that carpeted wall that your tape won't stay stuck to. Put the tape on the paper and the wall, and then put a t-pin through the corner at an angle.

Foam core board: This is for when you have a room where you are at the front, and the speaker is on the stage. Ask for three flip-chart stands with fold-down feet or sturdy hotel stands, and put that board up

on the feet. I bought my piece of foam board at an art store. It's forty-eight by ninety-six inches, and I scored it to create a trifold using a t-square and my knife. Don't go all the way through the foam core when you score it, just a little bit, and remember to understand that two scores will go on one side and one in the center on the other. Try folding a piece of paper first so you get what I am talking about. They used to score it for you in the art store but made so many mistakes that they don't do it anymore, which is why you should practice first. LOL.

That foam core has been with me all over the world. When it gets old and battered, I throw it away. To pack it for the airplane, I put bubble wrap over the top, bottom, and a little around the middle. Then I get two bags at the airline that they use for child seats and put it into them. Have the airline staff label it "fragile" and add it to the oversized baggage. You can also ask your client to provide a piece of foam core board or gator board onsite as well.

Now that you have your wall space or foam board, put your paper up on the wall. If you know that you will be drawing many illustrations, put as many layers of paper up as you think you will need. If you have sixteen-pound paper, you will probably bleed through, so be prepared to roll up the first layer underneath your initial drawing. But if you have twenty-pound paper, you can get away with using the layer under your first one and finding a way to use the black dots that may have bled through in your image. That's fun, right? This will make better sense when you go to draw for the first time as a performance doodler.

I also put my art materials out on chairs, a small table, or a tray stand used to take food off tables. I place those materials on either side of my drawing area. Some people use an apron with pockets or a bag attached to their belt to hold their art supplies.

Have all your materials out and accessible so you don't have to dig around for that perfect pen color.

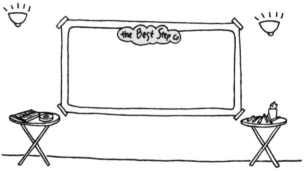

Open your pastels and have some tissues handy to blend them easily. Tissues are the best tool for blending. Napkins also work but are often too stiff to help you blend the pastels thoroughly.

9.2 Preparation Predicts Success: Prepping by Practicing with Live Presentations

Ready, set, GO! Yikes, the words come fast and furiously, and you are like, "Whaaaaa?! Stop! What did they just say?" That is the feeling during your very first sessions when you are doing live capture or running a Draw Your Future (DYF) session with a client.

Earlier, I mentioned the value of prepping by drawing while listening to the news or sitting in a meeting where you aren't presenting. Another great way to prep is to listen to TED Talks and draw out the content of the talk.

In some of my early classes, I would play a dog training video for students to listen to and capture. Michelle Obama also has a great short video on "Why You Should Vote."

Find and practice every day.

> Listen to the same talk until you feel confident with how to lay out your page and where to put things.

Repeating this activity will teach you so much—you'll learn about spatial arrangement, and you'll be ready.

9.3 Prime the Pump: Engage Your Participants in Advance with Materials, Hilarity, and Fun

When I facilitate an interactive drawing session using the Draw Your Future process, I want to make it fun. I bring materials for the group to draw with and provide weird toys on the table for people to play with. I also make sure I have silly things like a light-up wand or a sound effects toy so I can press "applause" at the right moment.

These materials on the table alert participants that this is going to be *different*! Yay! I even play music before we begin, during the breaks, and while I teach them to draw. Remember the basic shapes activity? I do that at the front while the rest of the group does it at their tables.

Then for introductions, as I mentioned earlier, I ask everyone to draw a selfie or their favorite lunch food on a Post-it and have them introduce themselves either to their table (if it's a large group) or one at a time to the room using their drawing. Then I place all those Post-its on a flip chart labeled "Who's Here."

One time I did this with about five hundred people. It looked like this:

So much fun! Now everyone's brains are warmed up, and they will be much better in the session—alert, attentive, and excited!

9.4 Listening for What Is Important: Training Your Brain to Synthesize and Draw What You Hear

People talk a lot, especially in meetings. Your job is to listen for the essence of what someone is communicating. If you don't synthesize what you hear, and instead attempt to capture everything said by every speaker, you will run out of space on your paper. Just listen for what's important.

> What's important can be defined as the core elements of what's being discussed or the nugget in what someone is saying.

Here you want to be careful that you don't take sides and only capture the things you think will build your case for change, but rather capture exactly what is being said. This is why, when you come into a room to capture, you have to clear out your opinions. Then you are ready to listen for the key essential elements in what the speaker communicates.

You can practice clearing out your opinions when listening to others outside of high-pressure situations like live graphic capture. For example, you have lunch with a friend, and they start the conversation by giving a lot of context. Just when you think you will lose your mind with all the details, they tell you the gist of what happened. If you were to illustrate this exchange, the context would help you understand the potential "scene imagery." Let's say they were on a hike, and it was a beautiful day (scene—trees, sun, etc.) when suddenly they ran into a

bear! They started yelling and successfully scared it away. Therefore, the bear and the yelling were the central elements of the story.

In a meeting, the conversation often goes back and forth as the individual or group explores a concept or builds the case for an idea or argument. You must listen and build the conversation into your imagery. Start by listening for the key elements in their current state. Such as the clients are being difficult, time-consuming, and not paying their invoices. What's at the center of this? The client is, so capture them first and build the elements of the story around them with a line connecting them to each element.

Eliminate your worry about capturing everything. It's not possible to capture everything, but it is possible to capture the essence. As a live illustrator, you must remind yourself of this constantly. Capture the essence of what's being said as if you have been asked to "just give us the key points." That's your job, nothing more.

9.5 Volunteering to Draw: Find Opportunities to Practice

The hardest thing is to jump in and start drawing, so you need to train yourself to break through your fear. Start small. For example, if there are meetings where you work, grab the whiteboard marker and start to capture the essence of the discussion in a picture.

If your meetings are on Zoom, doodle some meeting notes. Snap a picture and send it to the team. Yep, even if the drawings are rough and messy . . . because when you send them to others, you signal to them that you are drawing the notes.

As you progress, which will happen very quickly, you will get better at organizing your paper and chunking things together. Chunking is just what you imagine: putting similar comments next to each other. When you are running a Draw Your Future session, people will often talk about the same categories of things: "We have a high-performing team." "We collaborate." "We have fun." These are all about the central element of the team.

In some sessions, I ask clients to help me find the categories so I can put them in the right place. Inviting them to help by asking questions, such as "Where's that? Do we have that on the map already?" signals that this is their map. And people taking more ownership of it is a great sign because that means they will actually *do* something with the information.

9.6 Trust Your Instincts: Prime the Pump with Experiences

The key to being able to capture live in a room is to trust what comes to you. Once you put aside your fear about whether your drawings will be good enough, you will begin to see, hear, and sense both the tenor of the meeting and what you might draw for different concepts. Getting fast with this process takes time, so be patient with yourself. Review your maps after each session and consider different ideas for how you could have illustrated a concept.

Trust the first idea you get and capture it, even if you don't know how to draw it. Just do a quick sketch and go back and redraw it if you need to. As you learn to trust your instincts, you will become more relaxed and let the ideas come through. Prime the pump by researching the kinds of images used in this person or team's process or company. Review their website and practice drawing the objects they are familiar with, so they become second nature to you as well. Make online images your new best friend. Explore cartoons of concepts and practice drawing them to embed them into your store of image ideas.

You will improve dramatically the more you draw. That's the essence of getting better. Know that you have a tried and true process—Draw Your Future—that will be the easiest guide of all. Once you begin to run the process, you will feel secure in where you are going, and then the fun can begin when you find yourself drawing something you never believed you could. Let it be a fun exploration, push the critic out of the room, and let the creativity flow!

 CHAPTER SUMMARY
KEY TAKEAWAYS:

- Knowing what surface you will be working on during a session is key in preparing the best materials and avoiding any wall damage.

- Prime the pump by listening to videos and drawing what you hear, looking up images to draw, or volunteering to draw. Keep the critic out of your head!

- It is essential to clear yourself of all opinions before capturing what you hear to ensure that you truly capture what is important to the session and leave your biases behind.

CHAPTER 10

The More Positive, the Better

In my thirty-five years of facilitation, I have had and participated in many successful sessions. I have also been part of a few massive failures (ouch!). Almost all of these "learning experiences" had some common themes. Sometimes it had to do with the room setup—the room was too small or the group too divided. Other times it was because good ground rules had not been established at the beginning, or a leader lacked transparency.

But the most common misstep was unclear context-setting or not describing why (scientifically and emotionally) a picture is worth a thousand words and how you, as their facilitator, will help the team be successful. You are their guide, their scribe, their buoy when the waters get rough. You get the privilege of working with teams and demonstrating good listening to help them let go of the past and step (sometimes gingerly) across the chasm into their dream future.

10.1   Handling the Naysayers: Facilitating a Successful Session

In any session using visuals, especially when drawing the future, there are often those people who will try to revert to the "how hole" way of thinking. They throw their hands in the air, insisting they need to know how we are going  to do it to move forward. People spend years working on how they are going to get there, looking for the perfect plan.

Let me be clear. Your job, facilitating this with yourself or your team, is to remain positive and optimistic, no matter how frustrated you may become. I will often use an imaginary parking lot for people like this. I put their issues in the parking lot so we can talk about them after the session—because believing that achieving this future is possible is 75 percent of the battle. We can spend years in the how hole, trying to work out how we will get there first, rather than trusting and moving forward.

This is when having more pictures from a team or even the CEO can often make for a better outcome.

When people see their ideas built visually, it creates an unspoken buy-in and often leads to a more dynamic and creative vision that truly inspires the team.

Inspiration feeds perspiration.

Having more of the team's pictures can lead to a more diverse range of ideas, ensuring that the vision is inclusive and represents the perspectives of everyone on the team. Pictures build a shared understanding of the vision. When people see themselves and what they do every day in the vision, it creates a sense of ownership and understanding.

Additionally, seeing other people's pictures can help spark new ideas and build on existing ones. This can lead to a more collaborative and cohesive vision that everyone can get behind.

In one of my most powerful vision-mapping sessions, the CEO literally grabbed my pen and started drawing and writing all over the vision map. Once we had all the data, my team took it back to the studio and created a vision map for the company. That CEO had the vision map printed into a trifold with their vision, strategies, and goals all in that brochure. He brought that trifold into every single strategy meeting and spoke to it, referred to it, and highlighted everyone's role in making it a reality.

While you can find yourself feeling precious about the drawing you are creating in a session, it is owned by the participants, and the more engaged and positive they are about that future, the better chances of its success. Always hand over the pens when they ask and let them lead the way into a positive new reality.

10.2 Envisioning Your Future: Training Your Brain Toward Success

Have you ever noticed how easy it is to focus on the negative aspects of a situation? How a single negative comment can overshadow a dozen positive ones? This is because our brains are wired to—you guessed it—have a negativity bias.

This negativity bias is the psychological phenomenon that refers to our tendency to give more weight to negative experiences than positive ones. As a result, our brains have developed a heightened sensitivity to negative stimuli, which helps us to quickly identify and respond to potential threats.

This negativity bias can have a significant impact on your visioning session and its success, as we may focus more on the flaws and shortcomings of the plan rather than the positive and new direction we are heading. However, we know it is possible to train our brains to focus more on the positive aspects of anything.

> Your goal is to help yourself and your team understand the power of positive emotions when looking toward the future.

They make us more resilient, open, and collaborative.

Here is one of the biggest tips for achieving lasting success with the Draw Your Future (DYF) method. Train your brain for positivity by developing a gratitude practice, both individually and as a team. Practice intentionally focusing on the positive aspects of your work, your achievements (big and small), and your team. Actively express appreciation for them. By regularly practicing gratitude, you not only rewire your brain to focus more on the positive aspects of your experience, but you also demonstrate to those around you how to use gratitude as a leavening agent, reducing the impact and sway of our negativity bias.

Another way to train for positivity is through mindfulness. Being mindful is as simple as being present and fully engaged in the current moment—without judgment or distraction. By practicing mindfulness, you observe thoughts and emotions without getting caught up in them, which can help you break through negative thought patterns and focus more on the positive aspects of your experience and the people around you.

These are just a few ways to shift to a more positive viewpoint. Holding a positive intention about your vision and your Draw Your Future map will sustain your ability to persist until your vision becomes your reality.

CHAPTER SUMMARY
KEY TAKEAWAYS:

- Our brains are wired to have a negativity bias, which can have a significant impact on our success.

- You can train your brain to focus more on the positive aspects through gratitude and mindfulness.

- Your positive attitude will increase your resilience and help you achieve success.

Wrapping It Up
in Full Color

In 2024, in collaboration with Women in Cloud, we set a Guinness World Record for the most individuals in an online session creating a vision board—aka Draw Your Future (DYF).[11] We got emails from people around the world who were part of the event and created a visual representation of their future. They shared their dreams to be successful in their business or career, their desires for family and friends, for better health, and how they will be part of making an impact in the world.

Since that day, many have successfully achieved their goals. Some people share how they were able to make a significant shift or how they were able to let go of the past. Most of these emails are notes of gratitude for helping them believe that their dreams were possible and giving them a simple process to take action toward achieving them.

Whether you are a leader, manager, counselor, teacher, or someone who is simply looking to take the next step in life, I dedicate this book to you. I hope you find comfort in knowing that you have the power to change the course of your life, work, or relationships by creating a simple picture and taking action on it.

You can Draw the Future to . . .

Solve problems

Explain ideas

And sell anything

I look forward to hearing what you discover when you use pictures and words to describe what's next.

Thank you for reading, and thank you for all of the ways in which you serve the world and make it a better place.

Acknowledgments

When you write a book, the content and stamina to reach the finish line are fueled by others. Thank you to everyone who supercharged my day with their texts, emails, social media notes, and pictures, each filled with your stories that confirmed day in and day out that Drawing Your Future works.

Special thanks to Scott Ward for making my roughs into these beautiful and whimsical illustrations. Our ongoing creative thought partnership makes me a better person.

Shout out to Sunni Brown for who you are and how you expand the room with your ideas and presence and for offering me the gracious introduction to the Ideapress team.

Extra thanks to the Ideapress team including Rohit, Kameron, Jessica, Athena, Marnie, Megan, and Allison for your amazing work with my rough writing and concepts!

Thanks to my superstar clients both named and nameless for inviting me to help bring out the Creative Genius with you and your teams.

Special hugs to everyone at the DeBruce Foundation and extended team for your ongoing partnership and work to expand economic pathways for everyone.

Thanks to my beautiful wife Julie and our pup family for your inspiration, your belief in me, and your love.

Finally, thank *you* for taking the time to read and invest in your future self. May you connect with a vengeance to create the life, work, health, career, and love you dream of. It's only a picture and a bucket full of elbow grease away.

Remember, you got this! High five!

Endnotes

1   Meade, Melissa E., Jeffrey D. Wammes, and Myra A. Fernandes. "Drawing as an Encoding Tool: Memorial Benefits in Younger and Older Adults." *Experimental Aging Research* 44, no. 5, (2017): 369–96. https://www.tandfonline.com/doi/abs/10.1080/0361073X.2018.1521432?journalCode=uear20.

2   Daily Mail Reporter. "Why Ugly Fonts and Messy Handwriting Make It Easier to Remember What You've Read." Mail Online, January 17, 2011. https://www.dailymail.co.uk/news/article-1347058/Why-ugly-fonts-messy-handwriting-make-easier-remember-youve-read.html.

3   Krasniak, Michelle. "Visual Content and Social Media Marketing: New Research." Social Media Examiner, May 30, 2017. https://www.socialmediaexaminer.com/visual-content-and-social-media-marketing-new-research/.

4   Hershfield, Hal. "The Benefits of Getting to Know Your Future Self." *Wall Street Journal*, June 17, 2023. https://www.wsj.com/articles/the-benefits-of-getting-to-know-your-future-self-d3246744.

5   Matthews, Gail. "The Impact of Commitment, Accountability, and Written Goals on Goal Achievement." Faculty Presentations, Dominican University of California, 2007. https://scholar.dominican.edu/cgi/viewcontent.cgi?article=1002&context=psychology-faculty-conference-presentations.

6 Barnes, Taylor. "New Year's Resolutions: Why Do We Give Up on Them So Quickly?" Baylor College of Medicine, January 11, 2024. https://www.bcm.edu/news/new-years-resolutions-why-do-we-give-up-on-them-so-quickly#:~:text=Common%20resolutions%20include%20exercising%20more,goals%20are%20unachievable%20or%20idealistic.

7 Agile Work Profiler. "Agile Work Profiler—Expand Career Pathways v2.3B." Accessed September 5, 2024. https://www.surveygizmo.com/s3/5612828/up-your-creative-genius.

8 Parker, Monica C. "Why Daydreaming Is So Good for You." *Time*, February 21, 2023. https://time.com/6256541/why-daydreaming-is-good-for-you/.

9 Johnson, Brian David. *The Future You: Break through the Fear and Build the Life You Want.* HarperOne, 2021.

10 Cowan, Nelson. "The Magical Mystery Four: How Is Working Memory Capacity Limited, and Why?" *Current Directions in Psychological Science 19*, no. 1 (2010): 51–57. https://www.ncbi.nlm.nih.gov/pmc/articles/PMC2864034/.

11 Guinness World Records. "Most Users in a Vision Board Video Hangout." Guinness World Records Limited, accessed August 20, 2024. https://www.guinnessworldrecords.com/world-records/727653-most-users-in-a-vision-board-video-hangout.

About the Author

Patti Dobrowolski, author of *Creative Genius You: The Equation That Makes YOU Great, 9 Tips to Up Your Creative Genius*, and *Drawing Solutions: How Visual Goal Setting Will Change Your Life*, and illustrator of *The Game of Innovation*, is the founder of Up Your Creative Genius, a consulting firm that uses visuals and creative processes to help companies and individuals around the world accelerate growth and change. A critically acclaimed comic performer, four-time TEDx presenter, and internationally recognized speaker, writer, and business consultant, she has brought innovative visual and game-storming practices to Fortune 100 companies, government, nonprofits, education, and entrepreneurs across the globe. Patti holds a master's in psychology with an emphasis in drama therapy from the California Institute of Integral Studies.

Her large format strategic illustrations grace the walls of Nike, Mastercard, Starbucks, PepsiCo, the Bill & Melinda Gates Foundation, and the Seattle Space Needle, to name only a few.

Index

Want help with Drawing Your Future?

Let us help you up your creative game.

Email: info@upyourcreativegenius.com

IG: @upyourcreativegenius

FB: @upyourcreativegenius

TikTok: @upyourcre8ivegenius

LinkedIn: https://www.linkedin.com/in/patti-dobrowolski-532368/

LEARN MORE:

https://upyourcreativegenius.com/

9 781646 871674